MW00579862

Hospice

Hospice

*The End Can Be as Beautiful
as the Beginning*

BY
Rebecca Malcolm Schubert

AS TOLD TO
Jean Bayview

FOREWORD BY
Diane M. Jardine Bruce

RESOURCE *Publications* • Eugene, Oregon

HOSPICE
The End Can Be as Beautiful as the Beginning

Resource Publications
An Imprint of Wipf and Stock Publishers
199 W. 8th Ave., Suite 3
Eugene, OR 97401

www.wipfandstock.com

PAPERBACK ISBN: 978-1-6667-8246-2
HARDCOVER ISBN: 978-1-6667-8247-9
EBOOK ISBN: 978-1-6667-8248-6

VERSION NUMBER 08/31/23

People are made by God in God's image. They are all spiritual—"little lower than the angels" as the psalm says. They do not need to be given a spiritual journey or made into spiritual beings; all that is part of what they are already.

—Penelope Wilcock, *Spiritual Care of the Dying*

Lord, take me where you want me to go,
Let me meet who you want me to meet,
Tell me what you want me to say, and
Keep me out of your way. Amen.

This prayer has become known as the chaplain's prayer. The prayer is from Franciscan Priest Mychal Judge, who was killed on September 11, 2001, at the World Trade Center while he ministered to a fallen firefighter. He was a chaplain for the New York City Fire Department. He had printed the words of the prayer on a card to hand out to anyone who needed them.

Contents

Foreword

WHEN A FAMILY IS faced with the fact that someone they love is dying, no matter what age that family member may be, they can react in many different ways. Denial. Anger. Despair. Acceptance. Emotions can be a roller coaster ride for family members. The same holds true for those who are told that there is nothing more to be done for them and that their time on this earth is short. This is a very difficult time in their lives.

Enter the hospice chaplain. This unique role in the chaplain world acts as a midwife, walking with the family and the patient to the end of life just as a birthing midwife walks with a family bringing life into the world. The unique characteristics hospice chaplains need run the gamut from deep compassion, healthy self-differentiation, tireless energy, and a deep love of the deity they worship coupled with the ability to be that calm, non-anxious presence regardless of the deity the patient or the patient's family worships. For the hospice chaplain it is not about evangelizing the patient. It is about walking with the patient through the process of dying.

This short, easily readable book offers those going through the end stages of life, whether it is the patient or their family or friends, glimpses of what others have gone through. It can help take the sting—or the fear—out of the process of walking our loved ones home to those who have gone before them. You can sit and read this book from beginning to end in one sitting. Or, you can use the short chapters as daily meditations—or perhaps do both!

Chaplain Schubert, an Episcopal deacon, has over thirty years experience as a hospice chaplain (first as a lay chaplain, then as an ordained deacon). She has done a masterful job of culling through the many stories that touched her heart to offer the reader a wide range of experiences families have gone through. She also offers a window into her own role as a chaplain, a role she has carried out not as a "perfect person" but as an ordinary person called into a special role in this life. Families whose loved ones are dying, those who are dying, and anyone interested in exploring the ministry of a hospice chaplain may benefit greatly from reading these stories.

The Right Reverend Diane M. Jardine Bruce

Bishop Provisional of the Episcopal Diocese of West Missouri

Acknowledgments

I WANT TO THANK the following friends for their gifts of time by doing the first read of my stories. Without the gift of time to do the first reading of this book and their initial comments, we might not have moved forward. Linda Breytspraak is a friend, neighbor, and a professor emeritus at the University of Missouri at Kansas City. Sarah Sullivan is a retired environmental lawyer, dear friend, and mother of our godchildren. The Reverend Becky Chamberlain and I met as our ministries (hers as a parish pastor) crossed paths as we ministered to the same patients and families. Ellie Chapman, a pastor's wife and retired English teacher, did the taxing job of editing our grammar. Finally, my diocesan Bishop Provisional, The Right Reverend Diane Jardine Bruce who, after reading our final draft, immediately agreed to write the foreword for the book. I have asked myself how to thank such dear friends, and it is hard to find the words for such a precious gift as their gift of their time. Time is precious and we only have so much!

Thank you to my coauthor, Jean Bayview, who, after an initial meeting in my living room, agreed to help me create my dream. Without her technical skills and willingness to discuss, rethink, and discuss again, we never would have gotten to our goal.

Thank you to our husbands who have lovingly supported us as they read, commented, and listened, and as we discussed the many stages of our dream to write this book.

As always, a special thank-you to all of the many families and their loved ones who have welcomed me into their homes and into their long-term care rooms.

Finally, I need to thank my sweet family: Bob, Kim, Beth, Spencer, and Fletch, who supported me as I made the scary decision to change careers to live my dream! Thank you!

Introduction

Dear Reader,

Why this book? Right from the start of this little book I need you to know it is my deepest belief that there is *one God* and there are many paths to Him. My path is my path. Your path is your path. I honor your path and I pray you honor mine. My goal is to serve daily every spirit God puts in my path. But you must also know I am very human, and I am a forgiven woman. First and foremost, I am a child of God. I am my husband's wife and the mother of our four wonderful children and grandmother of nine beautiful spirits.

Most of my ministry has been as a hospice chaplain (or a death and dying chaplain) starting about eighteen months before my ordination, which was February 4, 1995. My ordination is in the Episcopal Church as a deacon. In the Episcopal Church the ordination service calls the deacon into the world to serve. Within the service of ordination of deacons, read from the Episcopal *Book of Common Prayer*, there are two passages I will never forget. First, "You are to make Christ and His *redemptive* love known, by your word and example, to those among whom you live, and work, and worship. You are to interpret to the Church the needs, concerns, and hopes of the world."[1] The second is, "At all times, your life and

---

1. Episcopal Church, *Book of Common Prayer*, 543.

teaching are to show Christ's people that in serving the helpless they are serving Christ himself."[2]

I took the words of the service of ordination seriously and went into the world to live out my call to ministry as a hospice chaplain. Never in my life have I run so fast toward anything or anyone as I ran toward my husband and chaplaincy (once I got started). As I reflect, all my life experiences have led to this path, from the call I felt as a teenager to my embarking on a second career as a chaplain. It is a blessing to be with families and their loved ones as they start the great adventure into eternity. As a hospice chaplain, I view myself as a midwife to the spirit! I believe the birthing of the human spirit into eternity is as holy as the birthing of a baby into this world. I have written a booklet about the similarity, titled "The Birthing of the Spirit." The human spirit is the essence of who you are, with all your experiences, hurtful and wonderful, rolled into one sacred life. No matter one's age, spirituality, or religion, all lives are to be honored.

When the physician or nurse practitioner shares with a family or patient that it is time to call hospice, the patient's (and the family's) level of fear automatically takes a giant leap forward. It is true that no one wants to die. And depending on the age of the patient, one can believe there is more to do on this earth. However, I have found many times the spirit of the patient is ready to let go, even if one does not feel ready. It is so important to listen to the patient. The patient speaks in many ways and sometimes with words. A chaplain watches the patient's eyes, and what the body language is saying, and listens to what they are hearing from the patient and what the family is observing. A chaplain can then provide focus on the patient's needs, *not* the chaplain's needs. This focus on the patient is paramount to me as a chaplain.

In this book you will find patient stories from the chaplain's view. These are shared observations from my experiences as a chaplain. While my experience was not fiction, I have taken care to change the story details to protect the experience of those I had the honor of meeting. Some experiences have been combined and others have been changed in different ways to convey the hospice lessons I wish to share with you. Any resemblance to actual events or locales or persons, living or dead, is entirely coincidental.

Why share these stories? When I am with patients, I often share one of my stories with the hope it might help ease their fears. It is my hope that sharing these stories through this book will prepare you and lessen your

2. Episcopal Church, *Book of Common Prayer*, 543.

anxiety when you hear the word "hospice" in relation to yourself or a loved one. And I hope you will remember that hospice strives for no one to die alone; no one to ever die in pain; for the patient to have control of their death (to the extent possible); and for loved ones to be welcome into the sacred space of the dying patient, if that is what the dying patient wants. Also, to know that hospice does not mean death is imminent but rather a transition of care that focuses on the patient's physical, emotional, and spiritual needs as they approach the end of life, which may be days or months.

The end can be as beautiful as the beginning. I have no idea what heaven is like. But I have an idea of what I think heaven is not. I am *positive* there is a next level of spiritual existence. Death is not to be feared but rather embraced as a holy experience of our spirit being welcomed into eternity. When reflecting on my own death, I am reminded of a question from a 2014 TedTalk where David Brooks asked, "Should you live for your resume . . . or your eulogy?"

Thank you for taking this journey with me. We are going to experience positive patient deaths together in this book. But, being realistic, there have been sad deaths too. I have included several of these deaths because sin is an equal opportunity employer. Some find saying, "I am sorry" or owning their sin is very hard, so they never acknowledge their faults. Others find confession is a door to a peaceful death and a walk into eternity.

—— *Chapter 1* ——

The Gift of Presence

PRESENCE IS A VERY important part of who we are. When I use this word, some might immediately think about physical appearance. The definition of presence I would like to discuss, though, is best defined as the quiet essence of a person who is just *being*. This is the spiritual self in each of us that, when in a comfortable space, shines through our eyes and face and can be heard in the inflection of our voice. On the other hand, presence is part of us that is hidden deep inside and is not available when we become anxious or nervous.

Another word for presence is hospitality. Henri J. M. Nouwen notes in his book *Reaching Out* that real hospitality is "not exclusive but inclusive and creates space for a large variety of human experiences."[1] I invite you to make the space that surrounds you as hospitable to your friends as the space in your home. Being accepting of others where they are, and not where you would like them to be, is true hospitality. Being hospitable and open to others is the heart and spirit of the gift of presence. As we start the discussion of presence, it is important to remember that acceptance and agreement are not interchangeable words.

So many times I have been asked, "What can I do to support a friend going through a crisis? What should I say when I see the friend?" Please note the pronoun "I." When a friend is in a crisis, and in need of emotional

1. Nouwen, *Reaching Out*, 106.

and spiritual support, it is important to realize that the friend's crisis is not about us. It is about the friend!

By our very human nature, it is natural for us to focus inward, making ourselves the center of attention. Please consider a new approach: The friend in need is to become the center of the spiritual energy. The person in need, by the nature of the situation, becomes the one on a journey, and we become the invited guest. As a friend, we bring the gift of quiet presence, available to listen and to sit quietly. In this situation, there is no need to share our story or to make our entrance one of note. Presence puts the one in need at the center.

When talking about the gift of presence, I once heard an older chaplain explain how, years ago, he had received a thank-you letter from a family he had been with in the emergency room. Over a long day he had to make several visits to the family as they kept their vigil. They thanked him for the comforting words and the profound wisdom he had shared. He marveled at their comments because he said, "All I did was introduce myself and ask the family, 'What may I do to support you?'" This family had received the gift of presence.

It is a hard gift to give! It is much easier for us, in our humanness, to talk about ourselves and not to listen. But people in need don't need us to *do*; they need us to *be*. Fight the overwhelming desire to share your story. Listen to their story with all your senses. Don't make any big pronouncements as to how things should be resolved but allow them to talk until they answer their own questions.

This is the true gift of presence—one that cannot be purchased and wrapped in beautiful paper. The gift of presence is a spiritual offering directly from the heart—a true treasure.

– Chapter 2 –

The Teacher

THE COMPLETION OF MY bachelor's degree was in sight and the only thing standing in the way was a six-week math class. The course was scheduled to meet every day, Monday through Friday, for ninety minutes with one break. To the university, this course was basic mathematics. To me, it might as well have been called "bonehead math," since even in its approach to the basics, it made no sense to me. Through my dyslexic eyes, math is a combination of numbers and characters that have been twisted and turned, made indiscernible as you apply needless rules and theorems. Spirituality, unlike math, is crystal clear for me because it is the essence of a person.

On the first day of class, the head of the math department introduced himself at the front of the room. He appeared tired and grumpy, a real curmudgeon. The strong cologne of cigarette smoke encapsulated his disheveled presence. He seemed past caring about looks and much more interested in the position of decimal points. With indifference, he announced he would be teaching this course. The other students and I looked around at each other, slightly puzzled at why the head of the department would lead "math for dummies." This was the sort of class a new assistant professor or teaching assistant would teach. He curtly announced he was retiring, and his intention was to end his tenure with the first class he taught when joining the department many years prior.

The lessons and the weeks slogged on. Math was already a difficult subject for me, a dyslexic, and the course was even more difficult than I could have imagined. The professor barely spoke outside the lessons, and he was routinely terse and, as I said, a curmudgeon. He never gave support or guidance in class. During our breaks each day, he would stand alone off to the side smoking. I did my best to focus on a passing grade, though his cues led me to believe all of us were failing the course miserably.

A few weeks into the course, the professor went around the room asking each of us what it was we were planning to do following the completion of our studies. I shared that I was on the ordination track in the Episcopal Church and my next step was training at a nearby medical center. The professor nearly laughed out loud, and I could feel everyone around me pulling away emotionally. I could sense their breath being held for fear of being too close to the chaplain. From that moment on, no one wanted to talk at break with the "religious lady." I grew accustomed to sitting alone during breaks. I found a nice spot to sit on a stone wall outside the building that offered a peaceful, shady, and semiprivate time.

We were nearly at the end of the course schedule, and it was a typical day. We had just started a scheduled break and I headed outside, anxious for fresh air and a few precious moments to myself. I had just settled into a seat on the stone wall when I noticed the professor was quickly approaching me. I remember being nervous as he sat down next to me. I remember asking myself what I could have done. Abruptly, he asked me if I was really going to be a chaplain. I nodded and responded that this was indeed my plan. He said he had a story he wanted to tell me, and he wanted my opinion. He insisted that I was not to share this story with any of my classmates and waited for my acknowledgment. As I nodded my head, I could not help reflecting on the fact that I had not yet been ordained and was not yet a chaplain. I wondered why he was choosing to confide in me.

He shared that a few weeks prior to the start of this course he had been diagnosed with stage IV lung cancer and was given four months to live. Leading up to his diagnosis, he had been admitted to a local hospital for a lung biopsy and had to stay overnight. Following the morning test, he was assigned to a private room. After the nurse got him settled, she informed him the doctor and the residents would be around with the biopsy results later in the day, likely after dinner. As he waited alone, he pined for his cigarettes. Minutes turned into hours, and soon it was evening. The doctor and his residents finally came into his room. The doctor quickly reviewed his notes and unceremoniously informed him he had terminal lung cancer and, at the current rate of development, had four months left to live. The doctor ended by asking if he had any questions. The professor said he was dumbfounded and shocked at the news. He could not think of a single question or comment. All he could say was, "No." The doctor and his residents turned and left the room, closing the door behind them.

Not one person came into his room until breakfast arrived the next morning. He shared that he had never felt so alone, isolated, and lost with his thoughts, fears, and emotional pain. He kept thinking the nurses and other care team members had to know the diagnosis he had just received. He wondered why they had not checked on him or asked if he wanted to talk to a chaplain. He knew he would have declined a chaplain visit but admitted that later he would have changed his mind and asked for a visit. He gravely ended his story and asked me to make him a promise. He made me promise that, as a chaplain, I would never let this happen to another person. I prayed I would never let this happen to any patient on a hospital unit where I served.

By this time, we were late for class. The others had already returned to the classroom, but we were still sitting on the wall outside. I was reeling from the conversation but deeply impacted by the vulnerable truth he had just shared. I gathered all that was within me and offered to pray the Lord's Prayer with him. He said no, that was not what he had come to do. He indicated he had said what he needed to say, and his request was now in my hands. He thanked me for listening, and we both stood and returned to the classroom. He resumed the math lesson for the day, and we never spoke again.

My math professor's depth of spirit has followed me around spiritually for many, many years. I don't know for certain, but I suspect he did not believe in God; he believed in math. Many times, I have found hospice patients will share their story. But I have always wondered why he chose me. I have obediently kept my promise to him. During my training, I served for two years as chaplain for the oncology unit. Throughout my assignment, I asked the nurses to call me anytime there was a patient receiving negative test results or sad news. I checked in on patients, listened and prayed with them. I continue to do this for the patients and families I serve today. If it feels comfortable or I know the patient's religious history, I usually ask if I may say a heart prayer and follow up with a Lord's Prayer we could say together. I let them know they can pray the Lord's Prayer with me or peacefully listen.

I certainly learned more than math that semester.

—————— *Chapter 3* ——————

My First Hospital Visit

AFTER COMPLETING MY BACHELOR's degree, I started my training at a local medical center. Our first week included all the key essentials to properly orient us to the program and prepare for patient interaction. We covered the basic business operations first. We had staff introductions, received parking permits, and learned about the many clinical units, common areas, and offices around the hospital. Then, we energetically practiced a variety of communication and interaction skills in preparation for patient care. In one memorable exercise, we took turns lying down on a patient bed while others stood over each one of us. It taught us how valuable it was to communicate with the patient at their height or level of sight. More important, we learned not to hover over them like Snoopy perching on his doghouse peering down to those below!

The following week, the training staff eagerly prepared name badges that would define our purpose and announce our presence in the halls of the hospital as chaplains. When it was my turn to confirm the information for my badge, the staff was bewildered at my request for "Beck." Not a single side glance, unapproving whisper, or bout of refusal would change my position. My badge had to read "Beck Schubert," and I could not possibly accept their preference to label me as Rebecca or Becky. At last, they conceded but insisted that I tell them why Beck was so important to me. I assured them that in time, as we got to know each other, they would understand.

With the business details and badges sorted, we received the assignments for our first patient visit. The moment had arrived to start transitioning my training into practice. There was a mix of fear and excitement. As I stood outside the door of my first patient visit, I made sure to confirm I had everything I needed. Patient information, check. Name badge, check. Perfect outfit, check. Finally, I was living my dream.

I knocked on the patient door with eager anticipation for the experience that would greet me on the other side. As I stepped into the room, I could see several people gathered around the bedside. Intuitively, I sensed the patient was the family mother and wife. I was immediately greeted by the obvious patriarch of the family who gently grabbed my arm, guiding me toward the bedside. He had the most beautiful white hair and kind features. In a soft, sweet, joyful voice he announced to everyone in the room that the chaplain had arrived, and it was time to pray. Before I could say anything, not even my name, everyone neatly assembled around the bed, holding hands, and positioned me right in the middle of their family circle. In a matter of seconds, realization set in that they were expecting *me* to lead them in prayer. Of course, I knew prayer would be part of chaplaincy, but it felt like it was more of a concept than a practice to which I was a party. The weight of their expectations hit me like an elephant sitting on my chest. I swallowed my breath and tried to calm my pounding heart. As quiet panic took hold, I could not think clearly, let alone articulate a cohesive prayer.

Many religious traditions get their prayers from the Episcopal *Book of Common Prayer*. As an Episcopalian I was well versed in those prayers. In a normal moment I could have recited prayers from memory. I wished I had carried the book with me so I could have read it aloud for them. As I privately admonished myself for not preparing a copy in advance, the patriarch brought me back to reality by gently motioning me to proceed. With a deep breath, I silently called on the Holy Spirit as I bowed my head, closed my eyes, and prayed the words the Spirit delivered through me. I then joined the family as we each embraced warmly and spoke briefly together.

After a few minutes, the patriarch asked if I could write down my prayer, believing my words came from a formal prayer. I could no more write down my prayer than I could repeat it aloud. I wondered how I would summarize the nature of stand-up prayer, but just as the Holy Spirit had brought me the words a few moments prior, I was able to explain that when a chaplain does a prayer at the bedside, the Holy Spirit helps the chaplain pray. Further, I explained, you get the prayer the Holy Spirit thinks you need for that moment. In his eyes I could see the faith he had in the chaplain standing before him, even before I could see it in myself. He said it was just the prayer they needed as a family on that day.

After final goodbyes, I made for my departure, assuring the family that I or one of my colleagues would visit with them again soon. I slipped back into the hallway, quietly closing the door behind me, and immediately leaned hard into the wall as my knees wobbled and my heart searched for a calmer rhythm. Over many days and weeks, I would visit this patient several times. Each visit added to the valuable gifts and lessons I gained from that first patient visit.

The Holy Spirit's gift to me on that day was the realization that I was not there to impress them with my perfect outfit, my new chaplain badge, or my power of prayer. While the first prayer was difficult for me, as I feared saying the wrong thing, the Holy Spirit provided me guidance. I learned I was there to get out of the way and let the Holy Spirit speak through me. It was important to me that my presence was sincere and not rehearsed or planned. I wanted to be present and ready to serve where they needed me. I did not want to read from scripted notes but to allow the Holy Spirit to fill the room and speak.

After this visit I realized I had made a colossal error in judgment. I did not have the perfect outfit that day. In my mind's eye, my black patent shoes with bows, white hose, and sleek black and white polka dot dress encapsulated my professional presence and role as chaplain. I could not have been more wrong. I was perfectly dressed for my role as wife and mother attending church on a Sunday morning or for a nice dinner with my husband on a Saturday evening. I was not perfectly dressed for my chaplaincy role. Through my appearance, I had unknowingly placed a bright distracting spotlight over myself. I needed to blend in, to emanate a graceful, soft presence that created space for trust, peace, and connection. After that day I choose classic colors and simple patterns for my attire to blend into my surroundings and allow the Holy Spirit to shine more easily.

I also learned that patients and their family members trusted my pastoral presence more than I did in the beginning. They knew what I didn't sense at the start: that the chaplain had arrived when I walked into the room. To me it was not a chaplain who had arrived. For a long time it was Beck, my husband's wife, and our children's mom, who had arrived. As I grew into chaplaincy over a period of months, my own pastoral identity grew. It was my prayer to carry that growing presence with me daily in each patient visit over the next eighteen months of my training.

Chapter 4

Lesson in Goodbyes

During the first week of training at the medical center in August, we were instructed to prepare a list of the three areas of the hospital in which we felt the least comfortable or capable of serving patients. I knew my top three immediately and was quick to share with the group. The instructors took notes and nodded reassuringly that they understood my expressed concerns and perceived limitations. Upon arrival the very next morning we received our hospital unit assignments that we would keep for the duration of our training. I was astonished to learn I was assigned to all three areas I excluded from consideration. One of the three areas I had been assigned was to the oncology unit. I was still grieving the death of my father, who battled cancer, and I was certain the emotional fragility I felt in my heart would be a challenge for me. I held the memories of my father's experience and the impact on my family close. My instructors sensed strength and influence from my experiences and empowered me to see beyond my fears and perceived weaknesses.

I reviewed my list of assigned patients and was relieved to learn I had only one patient on the oncology floor and set off in that direction. I tentatively approached my patient's door and quietly knocked. I took a long pause before proceeding through the doorway and into her room. Over the following weeks and months, I visited this patient every time she was in the hospital. She was what I would call a "frequent flyer" as a regular on the oncology floor. She welcomed me with kindness right from the beginning, and I grew very fond of her. She was a meticulous woman who thrived on the details of daily life. She had a terminal diagnosis of cancer, but her short blond hair was always in place. From all appearances she was a lovely wife and mother to her family.

On Wednesday, the day before Thanksgiving, we spoke jovially about that first day when we met months prior. When I asked her if she remembered my first visit, she quickly chuckled, "You mean the day you hung on the door?" We both laughed at the memory as we talked of recent happenings since our last visit. She was full of excitement over her family's plans to visit and the holiday dinner plans they had arranged. As our time together wrapped up, I wished her a wonderful Thanksgiving and shared a prayer with her. I let her know I was looking forward to seeing her on Monday and hearing about her time with family as I bid her farewell.

A few days later, after attending the Monday morning report, I started my rounds on oncology and she was my first patient. I could hardly wait to hear all about Thanksgiving, but her room was empty. Surprised, I went to the nurse's station to inquire about her, curious if she had been discharged and sent home over the weekend. Immediately, I could see grief in the faces of the nurses staring back at me. We had all grown to love this lady and I was saddened to learn from the charge nurse that my dear patient had passed away shortly after the holiday celebration with her family. She was with her husband and children the entire day, visiting and enjoying the holiday. The nurses came in to freshen her up and asked the family to step out for a few minutes. In the forty seconds it took for the nurses to move the family to the hallway, she was gone.

This patient experience taught me how sometimes people choose when to go and how long to stay. As a dying patient, she just could not tell her husband and children goodbye—it just hurt too much. It was my feeling that the Lord felt her pain and did not make her say goodbye. This was a lesson in how hard it can be for patients and their families to say goodbye.

This was also my first true chaplain relationship with a patient, and it was truly a gift. Educationally I grew significantly through this experience. I never learned if she was religious or followed any religious traditions. She never questioned me or hesitated in my presence. She accepted me right from the start and provided my initiation and first experience with oncology.

———— *Chapter 5* ————

Something To Hold On To

DURING MY TRAINING I was also assigned as chaplain to the AIDS clinic. As was true for all new chaplains I was still developing my pastoral identity, and I was learning and growing with each patient I met. While making rounds on the oncology unit, I got to know a very social, vivacious young man from Scotland. Danny had bright red hair and red freckles sprinkled across his cheeks. He was the prettiest young man you ever saw and was charming. Danny had an adorable personality that bubbled—even in the hospital bed when he knew he was dying. Danny had a captivating aura, and he was always surrounded by his close friends. When Danny's HIV progressed, two friends had stepped in to care for him but could no longer do so at home. Once Danny was bedbound, the AIDS clinic physician admitted Danny to the oncology unit. His two friends treated him like he was their son and were there with him every evening. They were wonderful to him. Danny also had lots of friends from the gay community coming to visit. Danny knew he was with us to die, and he was very open with me how he did not fear death. Rather, he had awareness of his disease and lived with confidence and true happiness each day.

I am not sure how Danny got to the Midwest from Scotland. I suspect he bought a one-way plane ticket to New York City and disappeared into the culture. When I visited him, Danny shared he had a rough childhood. Danny was a man who was born gay, and he had always known he was gay. He was easy to talk to, and we built a friendship quickly. We bonded over our shared Scottish heritage, my perfume, and prayer beads. Danny shared with me a few times that he thought I always smelled good. He even said how much he wished he could smell that good. The perfume I was wearing was a Christmas gift from my husband, just a few months prior. It was a precious gift to receive a small bottle of perfume because we didn't have much money for extravagances. I remember the wonderful aroma and only wish I could remember the name of it today!

Around the middle of March when I was visiting Danny, he asked if I would loan him my bottle of perfume. My immediate response was, "Why?" He thought it could sit next to his bed and smell good. I don't think I gave a response. After much thought on Danny's request, one evening I told my husband I thought I would take my Christmas gift and share it with Danny. He questioned my motives, wondering if I was going to give it to him permanently or if it was a loan. The next day I gave the perfume to Danny with my wish to leave it with him on loan to enjoy. I told him I thought he could enjoy it while he was staying in the hospital. He agreed that he would give it back when he was done with it. His two closest friends supporting him agreed, too, that it would come back to me. He loved the bottle of perfume. He left the lid off so the scent could fill the room.

Danny always needed something to hold on to so he didn't feel alone. When he asked me about prayer, I got an idea for something he could hold. Danny never said and I didn't ask if he was a Roman Catholic. But he talked about wanting to pray and expressed that he needed help praying. I had been given a set of Anglican prayer beads and I thought Danny might benefit from using them. At that point I had only one set of prayer beads and would be giving him my personal set of beads. He was the first patient to whom I had introduced prayer beads. He asked many questions about the beads and how they worked. I called my beads "prayer beads." This term helped me share prayer beads with patients who might be apprehensive about using a Catholic rosary. As I explained the history of prayer beads, I tried to guide Danny to a broad cultural understanding of the beads—they were holy by several religious traditions, not just one. The most vocal users here in the United States are Roman Catholics, but prayer beads have a history of being used over thousands of years and many religions. I showed Danny how the divisions worked and that he could pray each one of the divisions for someone or something. He loved it and embraced the prayer beads, holding on to them all the time. The beads obviously brought Danny peace.

Time passed quickly. When I had first met Danny, it was the beginning of spring, and it was now summertime. I visited Danny each day he was in the hospital. He was growing thinner and weaker by the day.

I was about to leave for a two-week summer vacation with my husband, so I went in to tell Danny I would be gone for two weeks for my trip. I told him I would see him when I got home, and if not, I would see him in heaven. We both agreed and said our goodbyes. Within one day of my actual departure from town, Danny passed away. It was in the evening, and I didn't get any notice from the hospital because I wasn't on call. The two wonderful men who had taken Danny under their wing like he was a child of theirs called to let me know. They invited me to officiate at Danny's memorial service. Danny had requested a poolside memorial service. Danny loved poolside parties and it was one of his favorite places to be. They planned to have his body cremated along with his prayer beads and were going to take his ashes to New York, where he had arrived into the United States. Afterwards they would send his ashes home to Scotland by sea. Unfortunately, I had to decline, letting them know I was leaving for vacation and would not be home for two weeks. I did offer to officiate the service when I got home if they wanted to wait. It was a very difficult decision and I had reservations. I could not delay my trip. Looking back, I am proud I said no. I had to create boundaries and maintain those boundaries for a reason. There was always going to be a patient in need, but I had to create time to rest and time for me to go with my family.

Danny's friends brought me my bottle of perfume. That bottle of perfume sat on my dresser for the next fifteen years. I never wore it again. My experience with Danny helped me realize the scent was too strong for a chaplain to wear. For Danny to like it as much as he did and always talk about it when I visited meant it was too strong and too distracting for me to wear. The perfume put the focus on me, and I wanted the patients to be the center. I switched to a softer perfume; a hypoallergenic variety gentle enough to wear around those on oxygen. I have been wearing the new scent for work ever since. When we moved to a new home, I lost track of that bottle of perfume, but I will never forget Danny's love for that perfume.

My assignment to the AIDS clinic was my first introduction to what became a very active gay ministry to medical center staff as well as patients at the medical center. Many peers and chaplain staff shared I was a very safe place. I learned all I could about HIV/AIDS and realized how important it is for all of us to be loved and feel love. No matter who you loved, life was all about being loved. Danny's life embodied the expression of love beyond the stigma of AIDS. He would often embrace me in a hug, and I cherished my time with him and his close friends. The first time we hugged, Danny leaned in, saying "Chaplain Beck, relax; we are not going to exchange bodily fluids, let's hug!"

Danny died holding his prayer beads, with our shared bottle of perfume on the bedside table. Over the years I have shared prayer beads with many patients and will share some of those stories throughout this book. The prayer beads are shared for support to help the user feel the Holy Spirit, God's presence in their lives.

— Chapter 6 —

My First Funeral

THIS IS A STORY about the first funeral service I led as a chaplain. The funeral was for a woman named Joan. She was a large, full-figured woman who had been a schoolteacher. She was in her sixties and had stage IV breast cancer that had metastasized. Joan came into the medical center for treatments and then an extended stay on oncology. She had a wonderful family that was always around supporting her. Joan told her family how she saw a chaplain every time she came in, and the chaplain always prayed with her and encouraged her. Joan shared a little of her personal story over our many visits. She was delightful to visit with, and we always prayed.

A day or two after Joan passed away, I received a call from Joan's family. Joan's sister called to share they were glad she was now at peace and shared Joan's appreciation for me. As we talked, Joan's sister asked if I would officiate at Joan's graveside service. I said I would love to, but I had never officiated at a service before, and it would be my first. The sister on the other end of line said, "That is okay, dear, it will be Joan's first too!" I will never forget her words. I was very happy to do Joan's service, and it was a wonderful experience for my first funeral. After the service, they handed me an envelope with twenty-five dollars. Since I had taken time off during my shift from the medical center, I gave the honorarium to the medical center. But my supervisor returned the honorarium and said he felt my prep time had been on my time so I should keep the money. I put the money away for something special.

A short time later I was browsing a church's gift shop. I was admiring some gorgeous prayer beads! I had just given my only set of prayer beads to Danny. I couldn't help thinking to myself how much I wished I could afford to purchase them but resigned to admire them from a distance. The lady behind the counter noticed my admiration so she pulled out the prayer beads and asked if I was a chaplain. I responded yes, I was indeed, and that I had not been ordained for very long, and that I was working at the medical center. She glanced at the beads and then back to me. She then placed the prayer beads into my hand and said, "Why don't you just take these?" I told her I would love to, but I couldn't pay for them. I thanked her for the offer, but she insisted, "I know you will use them." I could hardly believe it!

Chapter 7

A Chaplain for Adolescent and Adult Psych

THE THIRD UNIT I was assigned to during my training was the adolescent psych unit. At the start I was hesitant to take this assignment because I had two children at home. I was worried about the boundaries between work and home and the impact the unit would have on me. I was worried I would project "stuff" onto my children. As I reflect, it was a real joy to be assigned to adolescent psych. The patients would typically be on the unit for six to eight weeks, which allowed enough time to get to know them better. Some of the kids were there for substance abuse like alcohol or drugs. Others were there because they were completely out of control, acting out, and several were abusive to themselves. They ranged in age, maturity, and size as well. During my training, I had to learn how to do a takedown and convinced myself I could do one if I had to. A takedown is when you step in between someone's legs with one leg and at the same time place your arms under their arms. This gives you control in an emergency. It was interesting to do but something I never had to do!

Once a week for an hour I would lead a group session with all the kids. It was not an invitational session; it was a mandated session for all patients. We talked about spirituality, not religion. Religion was the first thing many new patients to the group would protest by saying in a huff, "I don't want to do religion." I would remind them we were there to talk about spirituality and talk about their beautiful spirits—which is the essence of who we are.

It was a challenge to get this diverse group of kids to sit down together for an hour one day a week. I was always looking for different exercises to help them reflect and explore their unique situations. For some of the exercises I would play music for them to inspire self-reflection. One of the songs I used the most was "Ring of Fire" by Johnny Cash. The kids wondered why I would choose a song like this for them to listen to. I thought it was important they realized the song was about addiction, not just alcohol and drugs but other addictions too. One of the things we talked about the most was that a "ring of fire" could be a term for any type of addiction, even an addiction to anger. This helped some kids talk through their thoughts in a new and different way. Over six to eight weeks the patient groups rotated but had some overlap, so I always had two or three songs I could use, but this one usually brought out the most responses.

For another exercise, I wanted to help one patient open up. This patient was a very quiet young woman. Tall, willowy, and beautiful long hair. You could easily look at her and wonder what she was doing in the unit. She didn't seem to fit the mold, if there was a mold. The staff shared she was there because she had been abused physically and sexually. She would sit in the group with both legs crossed and her arms crossed over her chest with her head down. She rarely looked at me or the others in the room. Her body position was clearly saying that she didn't want to talk! One Monday I brought grocery bags to the group with colored pencils and other art supplies. I asked the group to draw their face on the bag as they saw their face. Or to draw how they thought they looked to others. The paper grocery bags were to emphasize how we hide from each other in different ways and show only parts of ourselves. One young man drew a full bowl to express how he felt "people just take from me." Others drew their best depictions of self at their level of skill and commitment to the exercise. The quiet young woman, however, was an artist. She did a wonderful picture of herself; after thirty years, I can still see it clearly. She included her long hair, but her face had only one eye. The rest of her face was perfect. The one eye she drew even had eye shadow. I asked her why she only drew one eye. She said part of her didn't want anyone to know her. She shared how her one eye was hiding. She kept one eye because even though she was hiding, it was important to know she was always watching. She kept both ears because she was always listening, always on alert.

I suspect that people who have been abused physically and sexually probably hide a lot of things. When we keep part of ourselves hidden, it takes anyone a while to get to know us. I will never forget the way this young woman portrayed herself and how art was her expression of herself. It was an important lesson that talking is not the way everyone communicates their feelings. Using different forms of communication, like different art forms, drawing, or listening to music, can help us express ourselves in a way we are most comfortable.

When the young patients who had been abusing drugs or alcohol celebrated a six-week benchmark, the staff held a ceremony where the patient received a coin to celebrate their accomplishment. They would tell me, "I hope you never see me again, Chaplain Beck," and I would tell them I would celebrate that they were out doing wonderful things. However, there were several I did see again over the two years I was assigned to the unit.

One of the things I go back to often when I think about my time on the unit was how it forced me to be more aware of my boundaries as a chaplain, wife, and mother. One of the things I still do as soon as I get home from work is to change my clothes. I do not want to bring my day with me when I step into my kitchen where I start dinner and conversations with my family about their day. One of our daughters had such a hard time understanding why Mom would go straight to her bedroom when she got home rather than stop to talk or play. I had to figuratively take off my day, and I could best do that by changing into my mom and wife clothes. By doing so, I could take off "Chaplain Beck." I could then put on my "mom" clothes and be there for my family. It is such a habit that for over fifty years I still change clothes after work. Dinner time has always been a time for sharing. I think all my experiences during my training helped me to not project different things onto my family and not look for things in my children that I was seeing at the hospital. I was able to create boundaries that kept things very clear for me. My two older children knew I was doing adolescent psych, and it never bothered them. They even helped me find the songs I used and thought how interesting and odd it was for me to ask for more songs like those from singer Johnny Cash.

I learned another precious lesson during my experience with the psych unit, only this one came from an adult patient. There are some patient experiences that, as a chaplain, if I think about them long enough, I will have a good cry. I don't, but I sure do think about it, and this patient is one of those experiences. I was on call and received an urgent call. The floor nurse explained the patient's mother had just passed away and the patient was coming to our hospital from a fair distance away. The patient had been taking her mother's ashes to the cemetery where she was going to place the ashes on her father's grave. The caretaker of the cemetery arranged to meet her and was going to open a section of her father's grave so she could add her mother's ashes. When she got there, the caretaker told her she could not put the box of ashes into the ground. Instead, he said she would have to remove the ashes from the box and dump just the ashes into the grave. Neither the caretaker nor the daughter had placed ashes into the ground before. He left the daughter to figure it out on her own while he stood nearby. Well, in the Midwest, there is one thing you can always count on—*wind*. What neither of them knew was that if you are ever going to place ashes into the ground, you must have a watering can or water spritzer so if you have wind, you place yourself with the wind at your back and with your water you can spray the ashes as you pour them in the ground. The caretaker did not have water of any kind and obviously didn't help. When she started to place the ashes in the ground, the wind blew those ashes all over her. I later learned that the patient was wearing a light-colored dress and new white tennis shoes. The ashes covered her arms, legs, and her face, and they were in her hair. Her mother's ashes covered her from head to toe. The patient completely lost it! She and her mother had not been very close, and everything negative that had ever been between them, in her mind, was now covering her body. She was an only child and was divorced. She was alone with a lifetime of bad memories and no one who loved her to comfort her in that moment. It was as though her mother had the last insult, and it was devastating. She just could not find a way to deal with it and spent six weeks in the adult psych unit getting through the horrible experience.

Sitting with her was one of the best times to reflect on "chaplain presence." The chaplain doesn't need to do or say anything. I said hello and sat down by her side. If you are lucky with some patients, you get a chance to say, "God loves you." But I was not there to talk. I was there to be present. I sat and listened several times a week for six weeks as she dumped all the yuck out and cried her way through it. After six weeks, she did leave and returned home.

Chapter 8

The Tailor's Missing Spoon

I WAS ON CALL at the medical center when I got a page at 3 a.m. that a patient had died and a chaplain was requested. I was very surprised, since I hadn't been called to this patient earlier; usually she would have been part of my evening rounds. When I arrived on the unit, the nurse said this was an elderly Jewish couple. When I knocked and walked into the patient's room, I was greeted by an elderly gentleman sitting quietly at the bedside of what I immediately sensed was a very loved wife. I later learned he had been with her all day until she died. I was struck by how at 3 a.m. he was dressed in a full suit, tie, with his coat buttoned. Despite the warm spring night, he also wore a heavy overcoat and his homburg hat. He appeared to be a man dressed for business even in the early morning hours, to honor his wife.

I introduced myself and asked what family members I could call. "No one to call," he responded. I asked if I could call their rabbi, but he indicated he would make the call. He accepted my offer of prayer, so I prayed to God for both of their souls and thanked God for her life. Afterwards, I asked him to tell me about his wife. In a heavy Russian accent, he said somberly, "She was my life." He went on to share they had come from Russia when he was sixteen and she was fourteen. As though it was yesterday, he shared many memories throughout their eighty-two years of marriage. Before he could leave their home in Russia, his family required he must be married. Without hesitation, he married his good friend's sister, and they boarded a ship for the United States carrying a new sewing machine and a few personal belongings. After arriving in the United States, they made their way to the heart of the Midwest, establishing a custom tailor shop in the center of a bustling metropolitan city. For many, many years they sewed and tailored suits for the city's residents, including many uptown bankers and lawyers. From the very beginning they were committed to making their new home in the United States and understood they would never return to Russia. He somberly shared they never saw their families again and were not blessed with children of their own. Despite not knowing anyone and barely knowing the language, they bravely embraced what they had together and focused on building a new life and business.

I asked if he had any questions and he very quietly asked in his best Russian accent, "How will I sleep?" Perplexed, I asked him what he meant, and he said, "We sleep like spoons." Instantly, I knew what he was asking, as my husband and I also slept like spoons. I shared that my husband traveled a lot, so I told him that during those times I used a pillow either behind me or in front of me, so I did not feel alone. I suggested he try a pillow that first night. He nodded and said he would as we gathered their things to leave the room. I asked one of the nurse aides to sit with his wife's body while I walked him to his car. I assured him that I would go back and relieve the aide and sit with his wife's body until the undertaker arrived. I was aware of the sacred Jewish tradition to never leave a Jewish body alone. When we got to his car, I asked him to please let me know how he was doing, and he agreed. Unsure of his traditions, I was very surprised when he grabbed my arm and pulled me into a hug as he said goodbye. As promised, I waited until he left the parking lot and then returned to relieve the nurse aide at his wife's bedside.

A few weeks later while in morning report, the department secretary interrupted. She told me there was a man with a strong accent on the phone waiting to speak with me. I knew immediately who it was and went to a private area of the office to take his call. As soon as I said hello, he responded, "You need to know that the pillow, she doesn't work." He went on expressing how much he missed and loved his wife. Simply put, he said there was a hole in his drawer of spoons that he could never restore without her.

Over the years I have shared the pillow idea with others, offering it as a possible solution, keeping the tailor close in mind, knowing that sometimes a pillow cannot be turned into a spoon. Through this experience and many others, I learned as chaplain, I am not the fixer. I am the companion on the journey, and my role is to accompany and walk gently just behind so I am not directive. Even today I am struck by the courage that those two young teenagers possessed to leave their Russian home and travel to the United States to make a new life together.

Chapter 9 ─────────

Getting Control When You Don't Have Control

LATE ONE FRIDAY MORNING I was paged to the oncology unit to visit a patient named Betty. Before going into her room, the nurse told me why I was called. Betty wasn't eating, so the doctor said he wanted Betty to have a feeding tube. The feeding tube was going to go down her nose, which can be very uncomfortable. Betty had made it clear she was not interested in the feeding tube and would not allow the nurse to place the tube. The nurse wanted my help to gain Betty's cooperation. I was a little confused, so I asked why she was asking me as the chaplain to help. The nurse was convinced that I ought to be able to convince Betty. In my mind I thought, "Yeah, sure."

We walked into the room together and stood on either side of Betty's bed. The nurse had the feeding tube ready to go and began telling Betty exactly what would happen next. She said she was going to start with a spray in Betty's nose to help numb the feeling of the tube going in so that it wouldn't hurt. Then the nurse and Betty both looked at me. There was an awkward pause as the nurse nodded and said, "Chaplain." She was clearly prompting me to jump in and help. I did not know what to do, but I turned to Betty and said, "Betty, would you like to wear your glasses while the nurse places the feeding tube, or would you like to leave them on the nightstand? Which would be more comfortable for you?" Betty reflected on my question and said she would like to take her glasses off and place them to the side. I helped her remove her glasses and set them safely to the side. I let Betty and the nurse know we would move forward with the feeding tube and that is exactly what happened. I stayed with Betty for a little bit after the tube was placed. I told her it was a new fashion statement and we both chuckled about that. At one point she began to cry. I told her about my own experience with a feeding tube. I wanted to reinforce that it does not last forever and that it will be okay. We talked about the life-giving nourishment she would be receiving, and that the tube would stimulate her appetite and then the tube could be removed. We said a prayer before I left, and I never saw her again. She was discharged the following Monday before I made my rounds.

My main purpose being in that room was to help Betty feel a sense of control. The nurse realized it as soon as I asked about Betty's glasses. I think the nurse learned a lesson too that day. Giving Betty control over a situation where she felt she had no control gave her a chance to be part of the process. There was no question in her mind after asking her if she wanted the feeding tube placed with or without her glasses so that she could then move forward. We all need to feel a level of control in the most uncontrollable situations. It no longer was "Do you want a feeding tube?" It became "Do you want your glasses on while we place the feeding tube?"

I didn't know what to do when I walked into Betty's room. It was the Holy Spirit that gave me the question. I believe the Holy Spirit walks with all of us and sometimes speaks through us. My introduction to a deeper theology about the Holy Spirit came when I was studying for ordination. The Holy Spirit has moved through the Old Testament as well as the New Testament. The Holy Spirit is described in the Hebrew text using the female tense. The description speaks of the spirit as the wind that blows through us. The Holy Spirit as the female form of God has been the subject of discussion since the first Jewish Christians.

Chapter 10

Holy Space

It was my night to be on call at the medical center when I got a call that a patient had passed away. The other staff chaplains had just left the office and there was no mention of a dying patient, so I was a little surprised. But we all know God comes when God comes, and our job as his children is to always be ready. It was about 5 p.m. and the patient's family had just arrived at the patient's room as they heard the news of their wife and mother's death. The nurse said it was a quick change but a peaceful death.

The family and I entered the room together. The patient's husband was accompanied by his two adult sons. The older of the two sons stepped forward, acting on behalf of the family, urgently telling me they must say the traditional Jewish Kaddish prayer for their mother. He said it was tradition and he was upset because they had not worn their yarmulkes, a key symbol of their faith. Sensing his despair, I offered several alternatives with the smallest thing in the immediate vicinity being small bathroom washcloths. The family agreed the washcloths were the best option. I asked if I could stay and the husband said yes, so I stepped away from the patient's room to collect four small white washcloths, three for the family and one for myself so I could cover my head in respect. I had planned to step back as the family said their prayer. However, they asked me to stand right next to the bed with them. I passed the washcloths around as we each placed them over our bowed heads and the oldest son led us in prayer. At the closure of the prayer, they quietly removed the washcloths and passed them over to me.

It was over in what seemed like a manner of moments, but it brought peace to the family as they honored their wife and mother. The family said it was okay to call the funeral home, so I stepped out and notified the nurses. In the Jewish tradition, the body is never left alone. I offered to the family that I would stay with their wife and mother until the funeral home personnel came, but the older son said he would stay. I excused myself and checked in a few times until the funeral home personnel arrived.

I learned on this day that we can improvise even in the most holy of circumstances. We made do with what was available to us. Those wash-cloths served as a reasonable substitute for the traditional yarmulke. A chaplain comes to support all religious traditions of patients or their families. It's important that as chaplain I am there to be a spiritual presence. The chaplain is a gentle reminder of God's love for all his children, no matter their religious tradition or no religious tradition. God loves all of us. *All* of us! On this day, I was not there to be their rabbi but there to support and walk spiritually alongside them. A chaplain never comes to evangelize their faiths or practices. If you ever hear of or see a chaplain evangelizing, you need to call their superior. Chaplains are there to support your wants and needs, not their own.

---— *Chapter 11* ---—

Do Not Worry about Impressing God

I WAS SURPRISED TO get a page at 3 a.m. because, at the end of the day prior, all the chaplains had gathered to discuss their patients, what was going on, and what I needed to know for the evening. No one mentioned anything about this patient or that there was a patient that might be struggling overnight.

The patient was a woman in the intensive care unit (ICU) step-down unit. She was very frail, quite thin, and petite. She was suffering from profound grief due to the death of her only child. She was in tears asking to see the chaplain. I stepped close to her bed and got a chair so I could sit next to her, allowing us to visit face to face. I never like to "vulture" over patients by standing over their beds. Once seated, I introduced myself and asked how I could best support her. Tears just flowed and flowed down her cheeks. She seemed defeated by her grief and was clearly hurting. I can still remember her pain and grief as she sobbed. Finally, after a period of silence, she cleared her tears enough to say, "Chaplain, I need to pray. My daughter died, my heart is broken, and I need to pray. But I can't think of any words that would impress God."

I remember wanting to chuckle; it sounds "cheeky" I know; it was not the moment to chuckle. My response was, "Oh, dear lady, there are no words that you can say that can impress God. God does not want your words. He wants your love and your trust. Whatever you pray is just fine. It is more than okay with God. You can choose any words you want." She shared she was angry with God that her daughter had died. I told her it was okay to tell God she was angry, and that God already knows when we are angry. He always knows. I believe that sin happens when we do not admit our anger to God. I told her to pray with whatever words came to her mouth and her spirit. She still seemed at a loss, so I offered to lead her in prayer. We joined hands and bowed our heads, but she did not say anything. She was waiting for me to pray but I told her she needed to pray what was on her heart and I was there to support her. I told her to tell God she was angry and say aloud all the words she was feeling. She went on to pray while I listened and said, "Amen" right after she did.

This was probably the only visit I have ever had where the patient prayed and I didn't. Prayer is what she needed to do, and she needed me to walk with her emotionally and spiritually toward prayer, and listen, and support her. I gave her a hug as her tears continued to flow. I assured her that another chaplain would visit her again in the morning and that I would share what happened during our visit.

I have learned prayer is simply a conversation with God. There are no words that will impress him because he does not want to be impressed. He only needs our love. Open your mind and your heart and have a conversation with God. Tell him what is on your heart and know that he already knows your joys, your anger, your fears, and your dreams. He wants to share these with you and is waiting for you. Prayer is a great gift and opportunity to talk and walk with God.

Chapter 12

A Two-Part Reflection about the Holy Spirit

Part 1

WHILE DOING AFTERNOON ROUNDS on the oncology unit, I made a visit to a patient with prostate cancer. It was unusual to have prostate cancer patients on the oncology unit because it had been my experience that they were usually admitted to the medical-surgical unit where they would undergo surgery and return home soon after.

I gave my usual knock on the door and heard multiple jovial voices within saying, "Come in! Come in!" As I walked in, I was a little startled to see the patient had several visitors in the middle of the day. Most visitors planned their visits much later in the day after work. As it was, there were four men casually resting in chairs surrounding the patient's bed, joined in spirited conversation. They were all older men, and each was beautifully dressed in full suit, tie, and jacket. They appeared to be in their "Sunday best" from head to toe and really overdressed for palling around in the hospital.

I introduced myself as the chaplain, and the men seemed to sit up slightly in their seats, eyeing me more closely as I spoke quietly and directly with the patient. I let the patient know I would not stay but I would come back to check on him. He smiled, sharing he was doing well and expressed how pleased he was to have me visiting. I asked what I could do for him and he encouraged me to come back later that afternoon and hoped we could pray together.

Somehow the word "pray" caught the attention of the visitors around us. One of the gentlemen turned to me with a smirk as he mockingly asked, "You preach?" I was surprised by his question but responded, "Yes, yes I do." In a cheeky response, he asked, "What do you think gives you the authority as a woman to preach?" I sensed he was playfully provoking me, but without thinking or a moment's hesitation and having never uttered these words before, out came, "If a twelve-year-old girl can ride on a donkey from Nazareth to Bethlehem, nine months pregnant, and give birth to a baby in a stable, and wrap him in rags, then I think preaching must be a piece of cake." I stopped to catch my breath, shocked at my words, and instantly wondering if I had insulted them. I waited for a response. My words were greeted by a sea of smiling faces. It was clear they enjoyed my response, as suppressed chuckles grew into lively laughter. The patient spoke over the commotion, thanking me for coming and said he would see me later to pray with him. I thanked the gentlemen for visiting with their friend, adding it was nice to see them as I excused myself from the room. Once his friends had left, the patient did call me back to visit him. He never said a word about what transpired earlier in the day. He seemed to understand there was nothing that needed to be said. We both smiled and concluded our visit. I did not get to see him again after we visited that day. He had surgery and was sent home within twenty-four hours.

Looking back, I remember walking out of the room wondering where those words had come from. There was only one answer. It was the Holy Spirit. She was and is always present and I am always in her care.

Part 2

Remarkably, around the same time as this encounter at the medical center, I had the opportunity to preach on Trinity Sunday, the Sunday in the church year that celebrates the Trinity: God the Father, God the Son, God the Holy Spirit. As the priest and I discussed my sermon, I detailed my intentions to share my beliefs and refer to the Holy Spirit as the nurturing female part of God. Throughout my training and ordination process, I had shared my theology with my peers and with the priest where I was assigned. They agreed with my beliefs and supported me. As I prepared my sermon, the priest reinforced his ongoing support and encouraged me to preach what I believed.

On Trinity Sunday, the anticipation of preaching my theological beliefs had me a little anxious, so I arrived at the church early for the 8 a.m. service. Preaching our deep theological beliefs can lay us bare, and that was the cause of my anxiety. It was an early spring morning after a long rainy night. I walked into the church as clouds parted, showing the eager sun, and everything glistened with God's love. The rays of light shined across the budding spring flowers, causing them to sparkle in the mist. It was a breathtaking scene of beauty cascading that gave me a sense of peace, as if the world had been washed clean in the quiet spring rain.

As I completed my preparations, the priest asked if I was still going to preach the sermon we had discussed. I responded, "Absolutely," and he nodded with a smile, encouraging me with his full support, promising he would be right beside me if there were any questions from the congregation.

I preached about the Trinity—God the Father, God the Son, and God the Holy Spirit. I elaborated the belief that if there is God the Father and God the Son, then the Holy Spirit is the nurturing, loving, female part of God. I emphasized we often talk of the Holy Spirit as the nurturer who is forever with us and watching over us. I shared that I knew then as strongly as I do today that this is where my feminine spirit is reflected in God. And it made sense to me that the nurturing Holy Spirit is a feminine part of God. The moment I said the Holy Spirit is a feminine reflection of God, a loud clap of thunder erupted from lingering clouds and rolled through the sanctuary! I had to pause in the moment to allow the thunder to clear and to be sure that everyone heard me. It was then that all the men's faces spread with smiles and a few chuckles. The women looked on anxiously as my words were allowed to sink in. Every man in that congregation chuckled at "a female part of God." I completed my sermon and was shaking hands at the end of the service as several ladies eagerly asked if I was going to preach the same message at the 10:15 a.m. service. I assured them it would be the same sermon without a single change. By the 10:15 a.m. service word had spread, and the men were a little more prepared. They did not break out in laughter; they just smiled and shook their heads as my words washed over them. Mother nature did refrain from adding an extra clap of thunder in the second service.

I wholeheartedly believe both experiences happened through love, support, and guidance from the Holy Spirit. The Holy Spirit undoubtedly delivered those words about Mary through me in the medical center when asked about a woman preaching. And when I was preaching my sermon on Trinity Sunday, you would have thought my knees would have been knocking as I expressed my beliefs. Saying God had a female part was a big deal in 1995. I felt a lot of peace in that sermon because of the Holy Spirit. I was aware that it had become much easier to talk about my theology in my second year of training than it had been in my first year. Acknowledging to myself and everyone around me that I felt the Holy Spirit was the female part of God was a big step for me. Many congregations have grown in their theology in the decades since then about what women can and cannot do. Rest assured the Holy Spirit has been walking alongside us the entire time. She is always nurturing, always loving, always guiding. She is ever present.

—— *Chapter 13* ——

Being a Grateful Guest

AT THE TIME OF this story I was the chaplain for older adult ministries for a local medical center. I went to four facilities, each one for a half day a week. One night every other week I was on call. The first time I went to one of the nursing facilities, I met a sweet man who taught me a valuable lesson.

I arrived at the facility at lunchtime so I could walk around and talk to people. It was so much easier to get names and match them with faces in the dining room. When I walked into the dining room, I was first greeted by a huge platter of sugar cookies. I thought maybe they were preparing for a party. A staff member said the cookies were prepared daily as an afternoon snack for the residents to take back to their rooms. They put out a tray of different cookies every day, but sugar cookies were a facility favorite.

Right about this time, a gentleman walked up to the cookie table wearing very worn bib overalls. He stopped to grab a cookie and placed it into the little front pocket at the top of his overalls. Then he grabbed a napkin and stuck it next to the cookie. He spoke with the aide I was with, but she did not introduce me. They seemed to have a wonderful conversation and then he walked away. It was then she turned to me and said, "Oh, by the way, Earl takes a cookie every day and he keeps them in the top drawer of his dresser. Every couple of months we clean out that drawer. He never has any company but he takes a cookie every day so he has something to offer a guest should they visit. If you visit Earl, be forewarned, do not take a cookie." I quickly nodded and said, "Okay" without much thought.

Later I made my rounds, knocking on doors to say hello and visit with the residents. It was a small, older facility so I could typically visit all the residents in one afternoon. When I came to a door and knocked, I heard a deep male voice say, "Come in." I recognized it as Earl's voice and stepped into his room. I introduced myself and we talked for a few moments, when he looked at me with excitement, saying, "Oh! Would you like a cookie?" I hesitated and said as lightheartedly as I could, "No, thank you. You know the old saying that goes something like it's a moment on your lips and forever on your hips!" He looked at me as if it a took a minute for that to sink in. It became obvious to me and to him that I had just rejected more than his offer of a cookie. I had rejected his hospitality as a guest in his home. But he was so nice. Instead of acting offended, he continued talking. I knew I had really offended him, and I felt so bad.

As he talked, I learned he was a farmer and I quietly listened to his stories. Though, to be honest, I don't think I heard a word that he said because I was so upset with myself for not taking the cookie. I couldn't hear or think about anything else. After a short period of visiting, he asked if I would be coming back. I let him know I would be there every Thursday afternoon, and I would plan to be back to see him the following week.

As I came out of his room, I had not taken more than three steps after closing the door when the nurse walked up to me, looked me straight in the eye, and asked if I had taken the cookie. I felt I had been convicted and told her, "No." I told her how bad I felt and how I planned to take the cookie next week.

The following Thursday, I knocked on his door and he welcomed me in. He greeted me kindly and offered me a cookie. I could hardly wait to tell him I would love a cookie! I would have eaten that cookie even if it had mold on it! I ate the whole thing, wiped my mouth with the napkin, and placed it in the wastebasket. It was a beautiful, large, and thick sugar cookie and it was delicious!

Over the next few months, I visited weekly, and he shared more stories about himself, his family, and being a farmer. He was in his eighties, his wife had passed years ago, and their grown children lived across the country and rarely visited. I asked him if he had a favorite church. He said his wife was the churchgoer and shared he was usually out on his tractor from early in the morning until late in the day. He was out there all spring, summer, and fall with maintenance and other work in the winter to keep things running. He just never had the time to go to church. I told him I had heard from other farmers that, in a way, being in the fields was like church. They had shared feeling close to God being on their tractor plowing the fields. He completely agreed. He said he felt an amazing feeling in the quiet peace of the tractor going up and down the rows of the field as he planted. He knew God would send the rain and together they would grow the crops.

We had many, many visits and he knew I would visit every Thursday. After some time, he had not been doing well, but it was not to the point where the children had been called to come. Earl was still mobile and was able to move slowly with a cane. One Thursday when I arrived, the first thing the staff shared was that Earl passed away in his sleep, which we all felt was a blessing for him. It would have been hard for him to be confined to his bed.

I will never forget the look on Earl's face when I declined his cookie. For Earl, sharing the cookie was a gesture of hospitality. I was his guest, and he wanted me to feel welcome. As I reflect on it, I was saying no to his welcome to the stranger. Graciously, he welcomed me back and I was able to join him at his table with a cookie at nearly all my visits. It was my way of asking for forgiveness.

Chapter 14

Depth of Spirit

IN MY COMMUNITY THERE is a large Catholic hospital system that has multiple facilities, including two nursing homes. They were looking for a staff chaplain and invited me to serve. Never in their history had they hired a non-Catholic individual anywhere in their system, and I was the first non-Catholic woman (who wore a clerical collar) to be hired. When I got started, there were about 110 patients living in long-term care at the facility where I was assigned. I knew that many of the residents and their families were terribly upset that I was there. Many of the families came to my office to let me know I was not welcome, and I was not to visit their loved ones. I knew I was there to serve all of God's children beyond religious traditions and beliefs and handed it over to God. In time, many families came back to me with appreciation for my presence and care for their loved ones. But I knew their response was due to the prayers of my new sister and brother chaplains and, of course, the presence and guidance of the Holy Spirit.

As chaplain I had many responsibilities, including doing rounds on the units every morning, coordinating spiritual groups, and gathering patients for Mass and Protestant services several times a week. At lunchtime I tried to visit with all residents in the dining rooms. I cherished this time because I got to check how everyone was doing, and it gave me a chance to get to know them, learn their names, and discover more about them. Casual visits at mealtime also gave me a chance to see all the dietary variations.

How they were eating could be a key indicator of their health, and I could tune into each patient more closely.

During my time at this facility, I built a friendship with a delightful patient named Rosa. Rosa was a very petite, feisty, headstrong Jewish lady in her nineties. Straight from the Bronx in New York, Rosa was small in stature but full of chutzpah. She often spoke of wearing high heels in her feeble attempts to reach five feet tall. During our time together, Rosa was an excellent teacher. Rosa shared about her family and her Jewish faith. I want to share with you some valuable lessons about spirituality that I learned from Rosa and still carry with me today.

As a Catholic facility we held Mass multiple times during the week, including Sundays. One thing I always emphasized was that all residents were welcome at *all* activities, from church to bingo. But when I first met Rosa, her family instructed me that Rosa was not to attend Mass or the Protestant services. I could not quite understand her family's resistance, as many patients attended services regardless of their religious beliefs. But I had to listen and respect the wishes of the patients and their families. Each Sunday, Rosa watched my relentless bustling as I moved all around the facility with my volunteers escorting other patients to Mass. A few weeks had passed, and I had kept my word to exclude Rosa from my invitations. Then, much to my chagrin, it turned out Rosa had her own plan. One Sunday morning after getting other patients settled for Mass, I stood back to survey attendance. As I scanned the room my eyes caught a glimpse of someone positioned in the front row, middle aisle seat directly in front of the altar. Glancing closer, I realized it was Rosa. I instantly panicked and raced to her side knowing I had to get her out of there before her family came in! Once I got through the wheelchairs I knelt at her side and quietly asked what she was doing there, insisting we leave immediately. Shaking off my warning, she responded in her thick Brooklyn accent, saying, "You know, honey, your Jesus, he was Jewish! When I am here, I can hear the Old Testament, Psalms, and a sermon." She went on to explain that as she listened to the spoken word, she could close her eyes and envision being at synagogue. Every detail of synagogue and its familiar surroundings would come into clear view. After listening to her, I let her be and motioned to the priest and volunteers that Rosa was not to receive communion. Just as I turned back, Rosa's family had arrived and were livid! I quickly greeted them sheepishly, acknowledging that, yes, Rosa was in attendance. I confirmed that I was still very clear about their opinion on the matter. I shared Rosa's comments and that she would not be receiving communion. As they considered their mother's perspective, they shared how their next-door neighbor growing up was an Episcopal priest. He and his family shared their High Holy days with them and even invited them to attend midnight Mass at Christmas several times. In the end, they agreed to leave their mother where she was, and Rosa attended services many times after that.

Rosa's imagination expanded beyond attending synagogue from her seat at Mass. When she would describe what she was seeing and experiencing, you were a passenger on her creative journey. Once a week, I would gather with Rosa and a group of ladies from the facility. In one meeting I brought an oil painting and asked the ladies to develop a story of the scene. The ladies created an entire story! There was a big discussion about how many children they thought the person in the painting had and how hard it would be to raise so many children. We ended up going around the room sharing how many children each lady had. When we got to Rosa, I remember her tiny frame sitting upright in her small wheelchair, boisterously sharing, "You think that is hard—you try raising two Jewish children in a tiny rural area in the 1940s and 1950s! We had to build the synagogue!"

Several weekdays I found Rosa peacefully staring into the facility gardens from the terrace door windows. I watched her for several days before I asked what she was doing. She said she was "weeding the garden." Astonished, I listened as she added that her eyes would trace across the garden as her mind performed her treasured gardening activities. Each day when she went back to the windows, she would find that the weeds had returned, and she would have to tend to them all over again.

Rosa provided thoughtful insights to me as I made my daily rounds. One of my favorites came on a very snowy, cold Sunday. Many of the staff and volunteers had not made it to work that day because of the severe weather, and I had to do it all. I was stretched to support all the patients as well as gather them for morning Mass. Rosa watched as I hastily moved around the facility, encouraging patients to join the service. But very few wanted to leave the warmth of their rooms and interest was waning. I was determined and kept pushing my encouragement. After many passes by Rosa, she stretched out her finger and motioned me over. I knelt down next to her chair as she patted my hand saying, "You know, honey, your Jesus said to feed my sheep, not count them!" As was her nature, she wanted me to know I was working awfully hard to shepherd my flock on this day, and I needed to gain perspective.

As Rosa's life came near death, she became bedbound and was no longer mobile. I was visiting at her bedside when I noticed she was intently staring off through her window with a view of the enclosed patio. When I asked what she was seeing, Rosa shared there were three very tall, peaceful blue angels outside the window. I asked her if she thought the blue angels could come inside, and she said, "Yes, when they come inside, then I will die." When I asked if I needed to call the rabbi, Rosa said her rabbi would be called soon enough. Rosa died peacefully, and I believe she was accompanied by her blue angels.

Rosa will be in my mind and spirit forever. She was loved and she is missed. Rosa taught me how the depth of the human spirit is more important than one's religious traditions. She showed me that spirituality is not a religion. Spirituality is the essence of the soul. No matter how you see God, even if you don't see God.

— Chapter 15 —

Always Listening

I LEARNED A VERY important lesson on listening from a resident named Martha. Martha was a resident of a long-term care facility for about eight months. During her hospice stay, I would visit her several times a month. During our visits Martha shared stories from being a teacher for forty years. She shared how she had saved her money all those years to fulfill her life-long dream to travel the world when she retired. Martha never married, but she did have beloved nieces and nephews, all of whom lived out of town. Martha reminded me of her namesake in the Bible. She was the unofficial facility social director; she was always on the move.

When I visited her I learned not to be surprised if she had other facility residents in her room visiting. As Martha shared her life story, I learned how she loved hosting dinner guests in her home, teaching, caring for others, traveling, etc. Her life had been very full, and as a long-term care resident she continued her life pattern of hosting others.

When Martha entered the dying process, she immediately became non-responsive. Our nurses stayed close but didn't think Martha was ready for around-the-clock vigil. Her body had not given the signs of transition such as pooling of blood in the calves, discoloration on the toes or fingernails, or bluing of the hands. These are things our hospice nurses look for in the dying process, but they were not present in Martha. Yet, she was not responsive, or at least so we thought. Martha had stopped eating and drinking for forty-eight hours and the nurses asked me to make an extra visit.

When I arrived, I pulled a chair close to the bed and reached out for her hand. I held her hand, telling her God loved her. I sang every hymn I knew and looked up lyrics on my phone for additional hymns I didn't have memorized. I read Scripture and psalms to her, and I prayed a heart prayer closing with the Lord's Prayer. I was with her for over an hour. As I started to leave, I patted her hand and softly placed it back at her side and said, "Martha, God loves you so much." I put my chair back and started to leave the room when Martha said, "God loves you too, honey." She took my breath away. She had not spoken to anybody for forty-eight hours. And those were the only words she said. I remember thinking how she reminded me of the biblical Martha described in the Gospels of Luke and John. She was the type who would have been in the kitchen preparing a meal for everyone rather than quietly sitting at Jesus's feet. She would have been busy, but she would have been listening. I feel like the biblical Martha gets a bad reputation, but I believe she was listening! Just as this dear Martha showed she was still listening.

Martha reinforced what hospice professionals will tell you. Even when someone is not responsive verbally, it doesn't mean they are not listening. I think so many times the people who are considered comatose are saying things in their minds, and they don't realize they are not saying them aloud for others to hear. It just so happened for Martha that she did respond verbally.

I was reminded by the Holy Spirit that everything I say in the presence of the patient needs to be *appropriate*. I have learned to never assume that the patient can't hear those around them. Statements in front of a nonresponsive patient should be the same things you would say if they were fully alert and conscious. The space with a patient is sacred and holy. Even in the space of a comatose person, it is dangerous to assume the patient is not listening. They may be aware but not in the way you might expect.

———— *Chapter 16* ————

Choosing How to Die

FAIRLY SOON AFTER I became a chaplain in a long-term care facility, a lady came in to look at our single rooms. Marlene was in her seventies, and about six months prior to her arrival she had been diagnosed with breast cancer. Her doctor told her she had a year to eighteen months to live if she did not have any treatment. She had been very clear; she did not want treatment. She wanted to use the time she had to live on her own terms. Her husband had passed, and she told her doctor and her children her plan. She went home and made a series of decisions for herself so that her children would not have to. The first thing she did was to pick out our long-term care facility as the place she wanted to move into as she declined. Then, she did something she had always dreamed of doing. She met with a travel agent to coordinate a six-month-long world tour. She packed a suitcase and left to travel to each continent, visiting as many places as possible.

Marlene arrived fresh from her travels; she was now at the facility to pick out her room and confirm final arrangements. The facility was close to her kids, and she felt it would be a wonderful place to be. Before traveling she sold her home and planned to bring her bedroom furniture to the facility to make this her new home. The single room she liked was a large room and it looked out onto a busy residential street. Not a great view, but enough to see the weather and have daylight streaming in. She also let us know she would not be leaving her room. All meals were to be brought to her room. Marlene did not want to socialize with the other residents. It was important to her that the room she selected be her sanctuary for her remaining days.

In addition to bringing her bedroom furniture and other small pieces from home, she decorated her room with pictures she loved and replaced the curtains. Her room had her signature and was filled with beautiful things from her travels and prized possessions from her home. It was decorated such that you felt like you stepped out of the facility and into her home.

I visited Marlene daily between Sunday and Thursday, and she was with us for a little over six months. In our time together she shared stories of her life, family, and her six-month trip around the world. We became remarkably close. China was her favorite country to visit, and she brought a few treasures home that she kept in her room. One that was most precious to her was a small jade cross. It was paired with a gold chain and held great meaning for her. Before her death she gave me the jade cross. What a precious gift!

When Marlene died, she told her children that she wanted me to have a certain painted china plate and she gave another painted china plate to the volunteer that checked on her regularly. They met shortly after she moved in, when he was taken aback at how gorgeous her room was. He was the communion minister and would visit Roman Catholic patients with communion every Friday. Once he saw her room he really wanted to go in and meet her. Marlene was a Christian but not a Roman Catholic, so he did not have a reason to visit her. But he decided to introduce himself anyway and share his appreciation for her decorating skills. They ended up forming a friendship and staying close throughout her time at the facility.

Marlene is an example of a patient that "lived her dying." Marlene made choices—she made the choice of where to die, how to die, and what to have around her, and she allowed us to help and support her children. She was saving her children a lot of hard decisions. She made her plans very clear. As time grew short, Marlene knew her family knew her plans, as did the staff. Marlene was surrounded by her family and our staff as she slipped away. Marlene lived her dying exactly the way she wanted, and it was a beautiful death.

———— *Chapter 17* ————

One Last Breath Together

ONE DAY, WHILE I was working as a long-term care center chaplain, there was a patient named Marcy, whom I had been monitoring throughout the day. Marcy had her own hospice chaplain who would visit the center several times a month. But because the hospice team was not there full time, as the center's chaplain, I would visit with the patients each day. Marcy was no longer responsive, and the nurses believed she had entered the dying process. Fortunately, her family had arrived to spend precious time with her. I didn't want to intrude on their time together so I chose to make my visits short. I live by the saying "Chaplains come to visit; they don't stay for dinner." Throughout the day I would quietly pop in, asking if they needed anything and to let them know I was there to provide support if desired.

I was back in my office, when suddenly a nurse came running around the corner to tell me Marcy was dying. It was imminent, and they needed me "*Now.*" The family was in the room with her; the hospice chaplain had been called but had not yet arrived. I moved quickly from my office to Marcy's room. I gave a quick knock on the door and was invited in. There were five members of her family huddled around her bed. Marcy's son was holding her hand on one side of the bed with her daughter standing opposite, holding her other hand. Marcy's adult grandchildren were standing at the end of the bed, quietly watching their parents. As a Catholic family, I knew they would want to pray, so I asked if we could hold hands and form a prayer circle around the bed, including Marcy's hands. Now in position holding tightly to one another and Marcy, we bowed our heads and recited a "Hail Mary" and closed with the "Our Father" (or "The Lord's Prayer" as it is called in non-Roman Catholic denominations). We were concluding the last phrase, " . . . give us this day our daily bread and forgive our trespasses as we forgive those who trespass against us; and lead us not into temptation but deliver us from evil." Just then, as we prayed "deliver us from evil," something moved each of us to raise our bowed heads. Marcy drew in a deep breath and released it with a long and peaceful sigh, audible to us all, and she was gone! In that moment we knew, with the presence of the Holy Spirit, we had literally prayed her into heaven. And we each said in unison a joyous "Amen."

Marcy's family shared how they felt so much peace and joy in that moment. They were so happy to witness and pray with their mother as her spirit went to heaven. They felt it was the holiest of moments and a wonderful family memory for them to hold dear. Marcy's death was peaceful, quiet, and just as they had hoped for their mother and grandmother. They couldn't imagine not being there holding her hands tightly until the very end. I hugged each member of the family and affirmed how wonderful it was they were there with her all day and what a wonderful gift to be with her for one last breath together.

What is the takeaway from Marcy's death? Each death I have attended has been unique and sacred. No one death has been the same as another. We are all unique children of God, and we are all members of the family where we are all loved equally. When and how we die is just as unique as the life we have lived. No one death is more holy than another. In God's family there is no rivalry or playing favorites. Please remember that God comes to all of us! You can't go to a certain place to find God because God is everywhere!

Chapter 18

Believing Is Not Just Seeing

I HAD BEEN VISITING a patient named Tom, who was in the most unusual room at the end of the hall. It was a single room but was long and narrow. I knew from Tom that both of his sons lived out of town. One of his sons visited regularly while he was in long term care, but the other son was able to visit only every few months. They had different schedules, but he was able to see at least one of his sons on a regular basis. Once he became a hospice patient, they both came to be with him. I was not his hospice chaplain, but I was the chaplain at the facility, so I was there every day. The hospice chaplain came every couple of weeks.

I knocked and, as I entered Tom's room, one of the sons came to me saying his dad kept looking up into the corner of his room. His bed was along the wall, and he was staring up into the far corner telling his sons there were angels there. Tom continued to share that angels were looking down on him. He would reach out to them with his left hand. His sons kept discouraging him, trying to divert his attention away from the corner of the room. They kept repeating there was nothing there, and they kept asking Tom to lie back down.

The next afternoon, when I was visiting, the sons were upset because they could not keep their dad from reaching up. They said he kept reaching and pointing toward the corner, saying, "They are up there, right there, they are up there." The sons were frustrated with their dad. They believed just as strongly that there was nothing there. I finally asked the sons how

47

they knew there was nothing there. They both looked at me, very surprised that I would ask, because to them it was obvious there was nothing there. I replied that even though there was nothing they could see, it did not mean there was not something there that only the dying could see. I shared how I was convinced the dying have sight we do not have. I continued by asking wasn't it wonderful that their father could see angels waiting for him? What a blessing for their dad. He could transition from one life to the next with angels as his guide. The sons were not sure how to support their dad from that moment forward. I suggested that maybe they could say to their dad that the angels had not come to take his body; but that when it was time to go, they would want his spirit to go with them.

When we die, the body stays and the spirit goes. I shared with the sons that they were there as midwives to their father's spirit. It was a wonderful gift for them to be there with their father and to be present with him, to listen, learn, and share in his holy experience. The sons agreed and understood. They did not stop their dad from reaching out his hand toward the angels but instead encouraged him, letting him know it was his spirit the angels were there for. When I went back the next morning, he was gone. His room was already clean, and I never saw his sons again. Staff said he died during the night and the sons left energized. They talked about his angels to nurses and had a peace about his death in their hearts. They cried, but they also rejoiced. It was a peaceful passing.

As chaplain I have experienced dying patients that will reach and reach until they can't reach anymore. And then their spirit will go. After my experience with the patient in this story, I started sharing a wonderful Bible verse with patients and their loved ones during these times of need. The verse is Isaiah 41:10 and it reads, "Do not fear, for I am with you, do not be afraid, for I am your God; I will strengthen you, I will help you, I will uphold you with my victorious right hand." I encourage patients that, when they want to reach out, to not be afraid but to raise their left hand into the air to hold on to the right hand of our Father, who would hold them tight by his Holy Spirit. For loved ones, I encourage them to know they too are loved by God and that God will uphold them with his victorious right hand.

In fact, whenever you are frightened, or when you come across something that scares you, or you think you can't do it, know our Lord will hold you with His righteous right hand. Whenever you are in a tight squeeze or you are feeling guilty, the kind of guilt that you just can't let go, know our Lord forgives you. Hold his hand for a while until you can believe that in the depth of your spirit. This verse from Isaiah was shared with me in my own time of need. A Roman Catholic priest who was a friend of my father shared this verse with me many years ago. He was at a different parish from my father, but they were young priests in the community together. He was a wonderful person, and he was aware my father had passed away at an early age. He even attended my ordination service, which was very special for me. He gave me this verse because I kept expressing to him that I was not worthy. It was the end of my first year of training and I was wanting to stay an additional year because I did not think I was ready to leave training. I felt I was unworthy to be ordained. He pulled me aside and said, "Get a life, girl! God does not call worthy people. God calls people." He made me realize that if my father was there, he would say that none of us are worthy. We are all forgiven sinners and that is why we are called to serve God at the altar. Only one perfect person has walked this earth, and that was God's son and our Lord, Jesus Christ. We serve the altar out of our brokenness, and I was worthy because I am a forgiven sinner called by God. He told me he wanted me to hold our Lord's right hand because he would help me whenever I thought I couldn't do it. As my priest had said, "With God's help" we can do all things.

No matter who you are. No matter if you are Jewish, Muslim, Christian, or follow no religious tradition, God will still hold you with his right hand. Something we seem to lose is that the Jewish, Muslims, and Christians are all cousins. Cousins don't harm one another; they work it out. We are worthy because of God's grace. As in the verse from Isaiah, reach out your left hand and hold on to the right hand of our Father and he will hold you tight with his Holy Spirit. He is always with you and will always give you strength.

--- *Chapter 19* ---

God Can Be Anywhere

I HAD TRAVELED TO the Diocese of Texas outside Houston for a four-day Community of Hope retreat. The retreat brought together a large group of people to focus on lay visitors who make visits to church members who are homebound or in long-term care. The lay visitor course I would later lead is twelve weeks, meeting once a week with the goal of training members to visit other members of their congregation. The Diocese of Texas had a huge conference center with a large chapel, tennis courts, a pool, a lake, and other facilities. I was there with two friends, and we were together for most of the retreat. Between sessions we had free time we could spend as we wished. Frequently during breaks, one of my friends joined me at the pool, where we spent our time with our feet in the water visiting with other retreat attendees. Our other friend enjoyed her free time at the tennis courts.

After one of the breaks, all the retreat attendees came together at the chapel for a communion service. We were a large group, so we filled all the choir pews in the front of the chapel. I was sitting between my two friends somewhere in the middle of the pews. It was a wonderful service with a touching sermon. I remember sensing the presence of God among us as the sermon ended. As we prepared for communion, a beautiful hymn began to play called "Surely the Presence of the Lord" and it was holy. This was a hymn close to my heart and one sung at my ordination. The power of the Eucharist was almost overwhelming as we sat in that sacred and holy place. I could feel the prayer and the closeness of everyone as the words of the hymn were sung aloud.

As I listened to the words, I began to quietly cry and the tears would not stop. The tears flowed and flowed and flowed. And, of course, I didn't have any tissues! I turned to one of my friends, pleading for a tissue and she shook her head, no. I then turned to my other friend, saying, "I need a tissue, what am I going to do?" She turned to her tennis bag, but she did not have any tissue either. Panic had fully set in for me, and my friend seemed to sense my desperation. She reached into her bag, pulling out a sock and with a quiet giggle saying, "Here, have my tennis sock! I am so sorry; I just took it off!" I had no choice. I grabbed the thick, sweaty, dirty, and smelly sock and wiped my face clear. Its essence was far from the glory of our Lord, but it was all I had. I looked down at the sock in that holy moment and realized it made the presence of the Lord more real. If our Lord can be present in a dirty tennis sock, he can be anywhere he wants to be! As I was blowing my nose and trying to control my tears, the three of us began to giggle and could not restrain our laughter at the humor of a sweaty sock in a holy place with the Lord. At the end of the service, I returned the sock to my friend, and she stuffed it to the bottom of her bag. We left the service filled with laughter just as our Lord would have wanted us to do. Surely, we had been in the presence of the Lord.

It was an amazing thing that happened in the middle of the most sacred thing we can do as a congregation. We were together as Community of Hope leaders celebrating the Eucharist. There I was moved to tears by the beautiful hymn. In the middle of this beautiful moment the only thing I could get to wipe my tears and runny nose was a dirty tennis sock! I believe that dirty tennis sock was made holy in that space. There is a wonderful prayer just before communion that says, "Forgive me of sins known and unknown." That sock was a wonderful example of being forgiven of our sins known and unknown. Even in the dirty, sweaty, smelliness of life, our Lord is present!

I first heard this hymn when I was attending Cursillo. Many times in my chaplaincy I have felt the presence of the Lord in this place. The hymn reminds me that it is not because I am here but because I am representing God's redemptive love. That is what I trained for, to learn to be open so that the Holy Spirit could work through me. Even today, when I listen to this hymn, it evokes deep emotion within me. I feel the call of our Lord, and I know I am called to serve. Surely the presence of the Lord is also with you as you read my stories!

Chapter 20

Do You Have an Advance Directive?

THE MEDICAL CENTER WHERE I served as a chaplain had a group of cardiovascular doctors who would see patients in clinics all around the surrounding area of the metro. The patients would come to the hospital for their procedures and then go back to their hometown clinics for follow-up visits. One of the things the chaplain would do was go around and visit all the patients the evening before they had procedures. The main reason for the visit, besides meeting the patient and maybe the family, was to make sure they had an Advance Directive on file. If the patient didn't have an Advance Directive, the chaplain was to offer to help them fill out the correct paperwork.

Doing my rounds one day, I met with a delightful gentleman who was a farmer from a small community outside the city. I introduced myself as the chaplain and he said he did not go to church much. I said that was okay. Knowing he was a farmer, I said to him, "I bet being on the tractor as you tilled the earth and planted seeds well into some evenings, you probably felt close to God there." And that his tractor at times could become a very holy place. He smiled and agreed as he expressed surprise that I knew that. I shared that is how I would probably feel, and he was doing God's work feeding God's people. He shared that he did feel close to God on his tractor and thought that was where God felt closest to him. His church was in his fields.

We went on to talk, and I told him one of the reasons I had come by was to do an Advance Directive. I explained what it was and that if anything happened to him, we would follow his wishes on the Advance Directive. I emphasized it was good to know that with any procedure there was always a possibility that something could happen. He said he did not have one and agreed to start one with me, so we worked on his Advance Directive together. I encouraged him to put in his own words what quality of life is to him and to describe, if something adverse were to happen or he could not return to life as he was then, what he would be comfortable with. It was a lot to consider. He looked at me, pondering my words, and asked what I put on my Advance Directive. "Uh-oh," I thought to myself. A chaplain tries to never lie, so I had to admit I did not have one. He was shocked! How could I ask him to do one if the chaplain had not done one? He had me! We agreed that we would complete his Advance Directive that day and then at his six-week check-up, when he was back at the hospital, he would go to the chaplain's office, have me paged, and I would show him my Advance Directive.

As I went home that evening, I started to set my plans in motion. Sister Martha came over and my entire family gathered in my living room. It was my husband and our four children with their spouses, and together we completed an Advance Directive for my husband and myself. Then, just as he had promised, that patient did come looking for me and for proof of my Advance Directive. I was ready and had it in my purse to show him!

Chapter 21

Angels Are All Around Us

My First Angel

REMEMBER THE STORY ABOUT my first funeral? The family gave me twenty-five dollars for officiating at the service. I asked the people at the medical center if I needed to give the money to them since I did that service on their behalf as their chaplain. They said I could spend it however I wanted, so I tucked the cash securely into my wallet. I decided I would buy something I really wanted but couldn't afford on our budget.

Days later I was at the gift shop of our Episcopal church. I was walking around the shelves of flowers, cards, and gifts when I laid eyes on a beautiful silver and brass angel. You can't see her face, but on the card that came with her was a note sharing that she was turned inward looking at your spirit. I connected with her immediately and thought it was a wonderful thing for a chaplain to wear. I imagined how it could start meaningful conversations with my patients. I turned her over to see the price and it was exactly twenty-five dollars. I was delighted! And I knew in my heart the woman whose funeral I did would have adored this angel and been thrilled for me to have her. For exactly twenty-five dollars, no sales tax since they were a not-for-profit, I had a special new angel to walk with me on this new journey toward being a full-time chaplain.

This was the start of my wearing a necklace that would stimulate discussions with my patients. The angel was the first step toward wearing a

54

necklace that was not overtly religious but spiritual and had a story I could share. Around the same time my son asked me what I wanted for Christmas that year. I said I would love a board where I could hang all my spiritual symbols so I could easily see them and select different things to wear each day. He made me exactly that and hung it for me that year. However, I have outgrown it because I have accumulated so many pieces over time. One day I will replace it with a larger one, but today it remains very crowded!

The First Time I Shared My Angel

I was a new employee of a hospice group when I got a call requesting that I meet a patient at a local hospital emergency room. As it turned out, the patient was a nurse at our hospice, and she was being life flighted into the city from her lake home with a suspected cerebral hemorrhage. I immediately changed into my clerics, grabbed my angel necklace, and moved quickly to the hospital. I knew my clerical collar would show the emergency department staff I was there with purpose as a clergy person. It tended to help in urgent matters like this one. To my surprise, when I walked into the emergency department, my youngest son, who was in nursing school at the time, was working that day. He was moving quickly toward me in the large hallway. As he rushed by, he said a hasty hello and said he couldn't talk, he was heading to the helicopter pad to meet an emergency life-flighted patient. Before he whizzed by, I said I was called to see that very same patient. He was a little surprised but, realizing we had a shared mission, he enthusiastically invited me to accompany him.

I got to see the nurse come off the helicopter. I walked with her and my son to the neuro ICU where she was admitted. The nurse was not responsive, but I stayed and prayed with her as I waited for her family to arrive by car. They arrived about forty-five minutes after she did, and I stayed there in the ICU waiting room with them most of the night. Her father, mother, and sisters were open to my presence.

When I arrived the next day, I was able to go into the neuro ICU with the family. I learned from the staff that they had done a clinical procedure and the nurse was not responding to the treatment. Her mother and sisters were standing at the head of the bed, gathered on both sides holding her hands, so I found a space at the end of her bed to stand. The nurse was moving quietly around us adjusting her IVs on both arms—just going back and forth, continuously. With her family there around the head of the bed and the nurse doing his job moving between her many lines and tubes on her arms, the only part of the patient that I could touch to pray with her was her big toe. I touched her big toe and prayed quietly to myself. Moments later I think I was talking with one of the sisters when a nurse looked over and commented on my angel necklace. I thanked the nurse and said I wore it because I believed angels are around us all the time. The sister nodded and said she agreed. In that moment I had an idea. I asked the nurse if it would be okay if I took off my angel necklace and hung it on the IV pole. She thought it would be wonderful, so I did just that. That angel stayed on the IV pole until the patient was released to go home. She returned to work six weeks later! Can you believe that?

I went to visit her every day while she was in the hospital. I had my usual spot at the foot of the bed where I prayed with the family. I always asked before I prayed, and they were wonderfully supportive. At one point, when she had gotten much better, the staff asked if I wanted my angel back. I said yes, I would want it back when she was no longer needed. When that time came, she could return it to me, and it would go on to help other patients.

This really started the "angel gifting," with patients but also among the hospice staff between our two offices. Any time someone from the hospice team encountered a physical challenge, I would get a call requesting an angel. I don't think they knew that for each request I was locating more angels online and would order a new one each time. They were not always easy to find, but I could always find one when it was needed. I gave a lot of angels away locally and at our branch locations. I do not remember how many I bought, but I bought a lot! My large angel I loaned to several people with the agreement she would be returned when they no longer needed her presence.

My Angel Touched Many Lives

During the summer months when it is really hot, I do not typically wear my clerical collar, but instead I wear my large angel necklace or one of my spiritual symbols to hopefully generate conversation. I even got a smaller angel that I was able to add to a small silver chain so that she could hang nicely at my neck. I have angels of different sizes, but my favorite angel is the larger one, and it's the one I wear most frequently. There have been times when I loaned her out to others. Once, I was with a dear, dear woman who had been divorced but found her soulmate and a second chance at marriage. They were so in love. I got a call that her husband had been diagnosed with terminal cancer and hospice had been brought in. I wore my angel every day when I visited her, and she had noticed. Finally, when he passed away, she said she needed my angel. I let her know she could borrow her, but she would need to use her own chain and emphasized the angel was only a loan. She nodded acceptance and, when I handed her my angel, I said she would know when it was time for her to come back to me. I think she was on loan to her for six to nine months. After that time, she placed the angel in a little box and dropped her off at my office with a sweet thank-you note. It brought me joy to know my angel served my friend well and had come home at last.

Then, soon after, I had another dear friend who found herself in a time of deep sorrow. We had known each other for years. We were always there for each other, but we did not see each other very often as the years passed and our kids grew older. Her daughter and my sons were acolytes together at church. The boys gave that young girl a hard time and teased her like a sister. I think she was the only girl at that time who was an acolyte. When I was ordained, we were asked to have the banner that hung in our church carried in the procession. Each person being ordained would have a banner carried to show the church they were from. It was a great tradition, and I asked my friend's daughter if she would carry our church's banner for me, and she was delighted. In addition, I got to pick the carriers for the front cross and the clergy cross. The front cross was carried by my son and the clergy cross was carried by his best friend, another acolyte from the church. Our younger son served as a guard for his brother. They carried the heavy crosses with pride. Their arms were stretched as high as they could go with the end of the wood poles at their nose. When they played the hymn "Lift High the Cross," it just gave you chills watching those children. All four of them did a wonderful job.

A few years later, that wonderful young woman was killed in a car accident. I got the call during the day while I was working, so I called my office and let them know that I needed to go to my friend. I left early and went straight from work, still wearing my clerics and my angel. When it was my turn to talk with her, I took my angel off and placed it in her hand. I told her I wore the angel a lot and loaned her out a lot to others who needed her. I told her I was loaning it to her to help her get through her difficult time. I suggested when she felt she could not go on, to hold the angel as a reminder of God's love. I shared that the angel would walk with her and told her to remember that angels are all around us. Like many others before her I told her she would know when it was time for the angel to come home. I do not remember how much time had passed when the angel came home, but it had been about a year. That angel walked with my friend during the most difficult time of her life and then she came home to prepare for her next journey.

I continued to wear one of my angels a lot in my work. I was wearing my angel when I was visiting a lady whose husband was dying. After he passed away that day, she turned to me and said she was not sure she could get through it without my angel. I told her I would be happy to loan her my angel. Like the others before her, I said she would need to use her own chain, but that at some point in time the angel would need to come back to me. I took the angel off the chain and handed it to her. God and my angel had a special plan because this time the angel never came back home. One of the nurses I worked with knew the lady and said she wore my angel all the time and she would hold it in her hands. She really wondered if I would ever get it back. I waited about six months before I knew it was time to buy myself a new one.

I had several patients at a Jewish center in town and I always wore one of my angels when visiting my patients there. Angels have always been in the Bible, so I knew it would connect with my patients at that center. On one visit, a daughter was there with her dying mother. She commented that I always wore an angel and wanted to learn more about her. I said that yes, I wore her a lot, because I believe there are angels in the world. She thought it must be comforting for many to see the angel. I said it was and it was comforting to me too because it reminds me of the angels all around us. As we visited, she said she really wished she had an angel. She had recently been diagnosed with breast cancer and was looking for something to bring comfort while she faced her illness and at the same time was caring for her mother. I offered her my angel on loan, again gently removing the chain and handing her over. About six months later my angel arrived in my office with a thank-you note. The woman had finished her chemotherapy and knew it was time for the angel to come home. I started wearing her again the next day.

More time passed and I continued to have requests from staff for new angels. The cycle continued where I would buy angels and send them to my team members in need. I have each silver and brass angel blessed before sending it. This went on for some time. Two staff members in our branch office were let go because our hospice was bought by another hospice. I bought two more small angels with two chains and had them blessed before sending them to them. I wanted them to know the angels were always with them.

Through my experiences as a chaplain, I am more and more convinced that angels are messengers of God. I do talk to my patients about angels. I often ask them if they see angels or talk to angels in their dreams. I do this in hopes of bringing them comfort and telling them angels are God's messengers. Sometimes it is really hard for people to realize that the spiritual connection does not come from their body but from the spirit within them.

—— *Chapter 22* ——

And Let Us Go to Bed

THE PATIENT I WAS visiting, Theresa, was in a total care community. She was not communicating very much at this stage in her dementia. I did not yet know Theresa's story, but I knew she was Roman Catholic. Since I arrived during lunch, I sat next to Theresa so I could talk with her in the dining room. There was a nurse with her, and I had walked into a battle over food. Theresa had been told by the nurse that if she ate a little more, then she could go to bed. Theresa kept saying "bed" in response to the request to eat more and refused to take another bite. It was clear to me looking at her plate that she had eaten hardly anything. To engage Theresa in a different way, I encouraged her to say the "Our Father" with me and she said, "Okay." The nurse was on one side with a fork at her mouth. I started to make some chit chat with Theresa that she was not buying, so I went directly into the "Our Father" and we prayed out loud, "Our Father, who art in heaven, hallowed be thy name; thy kingdom come; thy will be done on earth as it is in heaven. Give us this day our daily bread . . . " Right then Theresa cut me off, saying, "And let us go to bed!" Exactly in rhythm with the prayer, she shouted her insistence on going to bed. The nurse and I laughed, enjoying Theresa's wit, but Theresa was still very serious. I thought to myself, "Okay, Theresa, you win." Even though she did not eat much, the nurse went ahead and helped get her back to her room. Theresa got to go to bed.

It is very common for a dementia patient to begin eating less and less. Their minds tell their bodies they don't need the food, so they eat less and less. For Theresa, she was at the point where she just wanted to go to bed. She was very clear and determined to communicate what she really wanted. And in rhythm with the prayer, she was able to clearly communicate with us. When the human body knows it is dying, it does not usually want food. However, there are some people who will eat a huge meal before they die. Hospice staff know that someone at death's door can suddenly appear to wake up and for the next twenty-four to thirty-six hours be alert, awake, and eat more normally. But then after this surge they soon return to the dying process. It's important to know the signs of the dying process and to honor each patient's desires individually. The hospice team will help the patient and the patient's loved ones know what to look for and shepherd them through the "holy process of dying."

Chapter 23

Everything Is Possible with God's Help

I WAS CALLING ON a patient for about six months, visiting her every other week. Betty got to the point where she knew my voice and recognized my face. Betty's bed was on the floor in her room because she tended to fall when she got up. Placing her mattress on the floor helped prevent falls. Each time I visited I would get down on the floor to sit next to her.

In my visits, I learned Betty had one son that lived in the area. He was attentive and came to visit his mother on a regular basis. Betty was of clear mind and she liberally shared her personal life stories with me. Along the way she had mentioned a sister and that she and her sister had not gotten along well in their later years. They collided like ships in the night. It was something that bothered her spirit and her heart. She seemed to wish they had done better together.

On one of my last visits to see Betty, the nurses told me before I went in that she was in a wonderful mood that day. When I entered her room, she was giggling and was just as happy as could be. I sat down on the floor next to her and a huge smile spread across her face as she greeted me. Her spirit was just soaring! I asked her what was going on, and it turned out her sister had come to visit. She shared how her sister sat on the end of her bed, not on the floor like the chaplain does. Betty said how she sat up in bed facing her sister and they just talked, and talked, and talked for hours. I was so excited for her, and I asked her how she felt about it. She said she felt at peace and felt closer to her sister than ever before. She said that through their talking, they were able to work everything out. She no longer felt the heaviness from her sister not loving her and knew that her sister did indeed love her. During their visit they shared stories of their parents and of their lives growing up as children. There was so much love, forgiveness, and empathy as they shared their experiences in family stories. It was magical. I remember thinking what a gift it was for Betty and her sister.

I listened for about forty-five minutes as she shared and went on about her sister's visit. What joy and peace Betty felt! At the close of our time together, we concluded with a prayer. Usually, we said the Lord's Prayer together and then I said a heart prayer. Betty wanted me to say a prayer of thanksgiving for her sister. We bowed our heads and held hands as we said the Lord's Prayer together. I followed with a prayer for her sister and gave her a hug as I started to leave.

After a visit with a patient, I always call the family member that is listed as the primary contact or durable power of attorney. Even if all I do is leave a message, I always like to make contact and provide a summary of my visit with their family members. This is a great way to get to know the family. In Betty's case her primary contact was her son. Once I got back to my office, I gave him a call to share a report from my visit. Instead of my leaving a message, he answered. I let him know that I had just had a wonderful visit with this mother. I shared how his mother was filled with so much joy and excitement because she had had a visit from her sister. I described how they were able to talk, share stories, and reconcile their differences. I went on about her new confidence, her sense of peace, and how they had forgiven each other and apologized for the years of bickering. I emphasized there was so much love shared in their visit with a real coming together of their hearts and spirits.

The phone was quiet. More than quiet, there was still silence. "Hello, are you there?" I said into the phone. He said, "Yes," he was still there, but I could tell something was wrong. Betty's son went on to say that his aunt had died five years earlier, and before her sister's death they had never reconciled with her. Now we were both quiet and I was stunned. We soon ended the call, but a little while later he called me back. He wanted to know what I thought of his mother's encounter. Could his aunt really have been there? I responded that if our God can make a rose, a hippopotamus, and a spring rain, anything was possible. It's the truth. With God's help, *everything* is possible. I told him there must have been help from the Holy Spirit to make that visit happen and to bring the great sense of peace that was in his mother's heart. I then advised him to not be surprised if Betty passed away fairly soon. He said he would visit her that evening, and he did!

Betty died within the next twenty-four hours of my visit. The staff said her death was unattended, but I suspect Betty's sister was there. Normally in our nurse visits they notice signs of the dying process, and then a nurse visits the patient every eight hours. Betty was very ill, but she passed with peace in her heart, knowing how much her son and her sister loved her.

To Betty, this experience was as real as the visits from her son. To Betty her sister was sitting on the foot of her bed like they were young sisters, giggling and carrying on. Only God and the Holy Spirit could have delivered this visit. Betty had a peace that passes all understanding. Betty showed how important it is to accept each other's differences, so we are ready to move forward together. Betty's heart was open to the Holy Spirit, and the Holy Spirit filled her with peace and joy. Everything is possible with God's help.

— *Chapter 24* —

Mary and Joseph

I STARTED VISITING A married couple, Mary and Joseph, in early fall. My first visit was when Mary became a hospice patient. Mary and Joseph were quite gregarious and lovely together. They were welcoming and so easy to talk to. Over the many months that I visited every other week, we got to know each other. Here is their story.

As always, I knocked on the door before entering. The answer was in unison, "Come in." I wore a clerical collar, and they were both a little surprised when they saw me. I introduced myself as the hospice chaplain. Without hesitating Mary replied, "We're Jewish!" and she indicated they did not feel they needed a chaplain. After we talked and shared, even with our religious differences, they were very open to my coming to visit. And that is what I did—I visited.

In my first visit with a new patient, I always ask if they need me to call their pastor or rabbi. I also let patients know that if they ever want to say a prayer, I could do that too. I ensured Mary I would say a prayer that would be appropriate for the Jewish tradition, but she still wondered why I would do that since I was not Jewish. It was important for them to know that, as a chaplain, I was there to support them. I was not there for me. As a chaplain I pray in the traditions of the patient, not the way I would pray in my private prayers. I shared with Mary that I was fine with where I was. I was there to support them spiritually where they were.

When it was December, I visited them about a week before Christmas. Mary asked me, "Have you ever met a Jewish couple named Mary and Joseph?" I shook my head. Mary and Joseph thought this was so funny and were tickled by this. Mary then asked me, "Do you ever wonder what Jewish people do on Christmas?" I was in fact curious and asked what they did on Christmas Eve. "We have Chinese food, and then we go to the movies. The only two places that are always open!" We laughed about it. Mary said her favorite Chinese food was sweet and sour chicken, and Joseph immediately said that he loved General Tso's chicken. A week later I was working on Christmas Eve and I was scheduled to visit with them just before noon. I made a special stop on my way and picked up their favorite Chinese food, along with crab rangoon and egg rolls. I had called the facility nurse ahead of time to stall Mary and Joseph from going to the dining room for lunch. I needed time to get there and set up the surprise for them. As I walked in with Chinese food on Christmas Eve, it made them just roar! They loved it! It was a very touching moment and brought them much joy.

Mary died in the spring. I went to her funeral. I would see Joseph occasionally when I was in the facility, but then later that year Joseph became a hospice patient. He had a heart condition that had gotten worse. It was obvious that much of his change was grief. Joseph's son and daughter-in-law lived out of town but would visit every couple of months. His daughter lived locally and provided day to day support and care for Joseph. While Joseph was in hospice, I really got to know his son and daughter. They were very supportive to make sure he had everything he needed. After each patient visit, the chaplain is supposed to call the durable power of attorney (DPOA) listed in the patient's admission form. Mary and Joseph's son was the one I called to speak with or leave a message. He was very open and appreciative of my calls. I called after each visit with his father and shared updates on how he was doing.

Joseph was a hospice patient for eighteen months. Eighteen months may surprise you, but Joseph was on a slow, steady decline. And as he declined so did the loud, boisterous laugh, and he became a very quiet man. I started visiting him every week. At one point we talked about calling a rabbi. I had asked him earlier about calling a rabbi, but he never wanted me to do that. Joseph talked a lot about the temple. He and Mary were very involved in different programs. He enjoyed sharing stories of the men's group and had a long tradition of serving his community. Joseph had owned a small intercity grocery store that was his father's before him, and he carried it on. He served his community by helping his neighbors out when they needed it, allowing them to take what they needed from the store and pay him when they could. After he retired, the men's group did a lot of cooking at the temple and, because he had been in the grocery business, they purchased the food wholesale.

As Joseph's decline started to accelerate, I started a weekly consultation with his rabbi. I told Joseph it was time to give her a call and urged him to let her visit. As soon as I said "her," he asked, "What? The new rabbi is a woman?" I said, "Yes" and that she was quite wonderful. He thought for a moment and decided, "Okay, have the rabbi come by for a visit."

After her first visit, the rabbi started visiting regularly. At one point, Joseph let us know he really wanted to go to temple for Rosh Hashanah, as he had not been to temple for at least four years. We got his wheelchair ready, hired someone to take him, and coordinated with the rabbi for Joseph to be met at the temple door and to be helped inside and settled.

When I made a visit the next week, with tears in his eyes, he said, "Beck, I have got to go to Kol Nidre." This is the day of atonement where you confess your sins and God forgives you. It happens on the eve of Yom Kippur. I called the rabbi to share his urgency and coordinate the details. Kol Nidre is handled by many temples through invitations only and tickets, so there was limited seating. It is a common practice among many synagogues to limit invitations to those who have maintained their pledges. Well, Joseph had not been paying his pledge for years; he had more than paid his pledges in the years prior when he and Mary were very active in temple. The rabbi intervened. She said if I got him ready and to the temple, she would get him into the service. And that is exactly what happened, and he was able to go to Kol Nidre.

Joseph died twenty-four hours after the service. We were all stunned. We all knew he was declining, but we were not expecting that; but we should have been. I didn't see Joseph again after getting him ready for Kol Nidre. I was honored when Joseph's son invited me to deliver the sermon at his father's graveside service. Since Joseph was at the age where so many of his friends were gone, it would be a small gathering. I told him I would love to deliver the sermon and asked about the rabbi. The rabbi said she would do the service, but since I knew him best it would be better for me to do the sermon. More than fifty people came to the graveside service. The entire hospice team was there along with staff from the nursing home. We all loved him and laughed, recalling how grumpy he was and yet remained so lovable.

Joseph really enjoyed the care facility, and he loved his visits from the hospice team. We became like family to him because we saw him so often. Joseph loved that we called his son after visits to keep him updated.

Here I was in a clerical collar, speaking at a Jewish funeral. It really showed that loving care and friendship can transcend religious traditions. I have had many other patients of different religious traditions where we grew to have deep relationships. We grew to not worry about our differences but to be united around care, meeting each other where we were. Everyone has a precious spirit. So many people don't realize they have a spirit. If we allow ourselves, love grows beyond our different views, beliefs, and traditions. We have so much in common, but we spend so much energy looking at the differences instead of embracing what we have in common.

Joseph's death was hard on me. The Jewish tradition is not always clear on heaven, but my traditions can also be gray on heaven. I believe there is a heaven, for lack of a better word. In my mind I am clear heaven isn't pearl streets and ruby buildings. I don't know what heaven is, I just know it is there. And someday I will hopefully meet all these precious spirits I have been allowed to shepherd while they were on earth! I can't imagine our Lord turning away Mary and Joseph! While I am here on earth Joseph will always live in my heart.

The details of Mary and Joseph's story were not changed from their real story and were told with permission from their son and daughter.

Chapter 25

Direction from the Holy Spirit

IT WAS VERY EARLY in my hospice chaplaincy when I got a call from the office that a patient was dying. They didn't share that the dying woman's children were not talking to each other and were camped out in separate rooms of her home. They just asked if I could go and see what I could do.

I arrived and the patient was not responsive; she was lying on a bed positioned in the middle of the great room. Her four children had each taken a different room of her home with their families. All were waiting separately to see what was happening with their mom. They were not interacting with one another. What to do, I wondered. Within moments of my arrival, I went to each room, inviting each child and their family to gather around their mom's bed. It was not an easy task as they did not all want to come. But in the end they all came.

As they gathered around the bedside, I started with the oldest child and asked him to tell a story about his mom. He was reluctant standing before his siblings and his unresponsive mom, but he shared a story. Upon completion of the story, one of his siblings said that the story went differently in his mind and told his version of the story. Then we went to the next sibling to tell a story they remembered about Mom. Soon enough, everybody was laughing and smiling, recalling stories from their youth. All the tension appeared to evaporate, and all at once they were a family again around Mom's bed. They told stories for a good forty-five minutes together. Everybody had really loosened up, and the mood was much lighter. At a natural break I brought the attention back to their mother and offered that we join hands and say the "Our Father" and "Hail Mary" prayers together. Those next to Mom placed a hand on Mom's shoulder so we had a complete circle of prayer with the young children included, and everyone held hands. I said the "Hail Mary," and everyone joined in the prayers together. I closed with "The Lord bless and keep us and make his face to shine upon us this day and always, Amen." About this time, Mom's eyes flipped open, and she asked me, "Are you about to leave?" I was astounded. The unresponsive Mom had been listening the entire time, and she suddenly was alert. I responded that yes, I was about to leave, and I let her know her family was there around her. She thanked me for being there, and I said my goodbyes.

This patient woke up and lived six more weeks. Her children put away their resentments and the tensions that kept them in separate rooms. They tended to their mother and loved on her for six more weeks. They were a family unit again for the rest of her life. I believe the Holy Spirit was there, and she is good!

It was a teaching moment for them and for me as chaplain. If they could find a way to ease up and laugh as a family, then what made them so upset could melt like a Popsicle in the summer sun. Their mom was connecting them through stories, laughter, and memories. It brought them back together as a family. They did not know what to do, and in that moment the family simply needed direction. I was able to provide them direction and, with something as simple as shared stories, they all relaxed and were able to take advantage of the time together as a family. It was hard to know what came between them as a family. It could have been a single moment they were mad about, angst over what to do, or even how to decide who would take the lead. Having a chaplain there to lead and give them permission to take over through their stories, they were able to find their way. In the end, it was not important what the tension was but that they came together for their mother. Mom was at peace knowing they were a family again.

Chapter 26

Letting Go

I HAD A HOSPICE patient named Lilly who lived at a long-term care facility. Lilly was the sweetest woman. She was in her nineties and was a patient for a few months. Lilly and her late husband had six daughters who were all married with their own children. I told her she had a basketball team at five daughters, but she said, "Yes, but you have to have a sub!" All her children and grandchildren lived in the immediate area. Lilly's family was so large that they would host family Thanksgivings in the church basement! Everyone would bring food to share and sit around the large tables.

When she started to decline, I began visiting her every day. During my visits there was always at least one family member with her. The nurse shared that Lilly's body showed signs she had entered the dying process. Lilly did not want any food and would get upset when someone tried to get her to eat. The nurse explained to the family that she was still drinking liquids but, once she stopped drinking liquids, the hospice team would start one-on-one care.

Several more days into the following week I was still visiting every day. It was then that she suddenly stopped drinking fluids and was no longer responsive. When the family learned from the nurse that she had moved into the active dying process, they decided one of them would stay with her all day and night. There was always at least one of her daughters there with her children. They would switch off and share time with their mother.

It was Friday afternoon, and I was making my final visit before the weekend. There were so many family members in the room that they were spilling out into the hallway. Lilly had not been responsive for several days. The oldest daughter pulled me aside to ask, "Chaplain Beck, what do we need to do? Is there anything we are not doing that we need to do so Mom knows it's okay to go?" I said, "Please don't tell your mother it is okay to go." I suggested telling her mother, "You are loved. We love you so very much and we will miss you. We will be okay." I said she could tell her mother that they were together, they had each other, and they were a strong family. She nodded that she understood and went back into her mother's room to share with her sisters.

All the daughters got together around their mother's bed, and they took turns saying, "Mom, we will be okay, we love you and we will miss you." Some time passed as they quietly sat beside their mother's bed. I was about to leave the building when the oldest daughter came back out to find me. She told me they had decided to take a short break as a family. They were all going to walk across the street to a small restaurant for dinner and then they would come back as quickly as they could. They thought it was still early for dinner, so that meant they could get a table big enough for everyone and be back within an hour. I agreed to stay and let them know I would let their mother know I was there and was nearby, but I would not stay in the room. I felt Lilly could use some alone time. The daughter thanked me and returned to her mother's room to let her know they were leaving for dinner but would be back very soon. The entire family ceremoniously picked up all their stuff and headed across the street for dinner. They hadn't gotten farther than across the street and approaching the door of the restaurant when I went in to check on their mother. Lilly had probably been in the room alone for only five to ten minutes when she had quietly passed away.

Lilly waited to pass until after her family spent all that time with her at her bedside. The nurse asked me why this would happen. I shared that in my experience for a parent with strong ties to their family—a loving, nurturing family—it is really hard to say goodbye and leave. No one will watch over those children better than Lilly, and it was hard for her to leave. Even though she wasn't responsive, she knew her family had been there and that they had left to go to dinner together. I have long believed that patients, even when unresponsive, are probably hearing and even responding to us even if we do not see or hear the response.

In the moments that followed, the staff and I thought that the family had probably just been seated to dinner and we had a little time before they would return. The nurse decided to give Lilly a bath, what we called an "angel bath," to clean her up a bit to prepare for the return of the family. In a long-term care setting, several aides will come together to give the patient a complete bed bath, put clean clothes on the patient, and ask the family if they want to send them off wearing anything special. The facility staff want to help with the angel baths and see it as a privilege to do so. Then they usually do something that I always chuckle at. They open the window maybe six inches or so, regardless of the season. They want to be able to let the spirit out. It was part of their ritual.

After the bath, I called the oldest daughter to share that her mother was gone. Her spirit had left the earth and was now with God. I let her know they could come back right away, or I could sit with her, and they could finish their meal. They chose to finish their meal and walked back together a little while later. When they got back, everyone gathered, and we made a circle around the bed with everyone holding hands. There were so many people in that small room that we made a very interesting circle, but we were connected to one another. We said the Lord's Prayer together, and I said a heart prayer. Then we dispersed with lots of hugging and kissing among the family. The oldest daughter said she and her husband would wait for the funeral home and I could go on home.

It was a wonderful experience because this huge family of children and grandchildren with all ages, including babies, were a constant presence around this woman. They were loving, caring, and committed to each other. They seemed to have accomplished something that many of us find hard to do; they had allowed each other to walk their own paths and loved each other as they were. There was so much love in Lilly's room. I think that said so much about the matriarch of the family.

Lilly had hospice staff with her for four days around the clock in what we called "vigiling." There was an aid, nurse, social worker, or chaplain with her twenty-four/seven. And there was at least one family member by her side too. We never want to leave a patient alone, even if they are nonresponsive. Sometimes we play music, read the Bible, have the family hold hands with the patient and let the patient know they are there. Occasionally, the patient will squeeze their hand. It is important to spend time with your loved ones, even if they are not responding to you. I encourage families to do this. If there is a living spouse, I often recommend for the family to give them alone time with their dying spouse and I even encourage spouses to get in bed and hold their loved one. It is important to know your loved ones are aware of your presence and they aren't alone.

Lilly did not want to leave the party! She loved her family so much, and they were all there with her. When they told her they were going across the street for dinner, she knew exactly where they were going and how long they would be there. It was easier for Lilly to leave in that moment than to leave with her entire family watching.

Chapter 27

Be Present

I RECEIVED A CALL from the hospice nurse about a patient who was no longer responsive and whose daughter needed support. I finished the visit I was making and headed to the long-term care facility. The patient's daughter had already arrived, and I joined her as we sat in her mother's room. We sat on either side of the patient's bed. The daughter started sharing stories about her mother and reliving memories and favorite moments. At one point during our conversation, the daughter turned her attention away from her mother and looked over to me. She wanted to know if I thought her mother could hear us. With confidence I affirmed something that I have long believed and have witnessed to be true. I shared that hearing and awareness of others is one of the last things to go during the dying process. The daughter was not convinced. She was sure her mother had no idea she was there, and her efforts to connect were falling on deaf ears. It was easy to understand the daughter's point of view because her mother was not providing any physical signs or feedback. I continued to affirm my experience and gently encouraged her to understand and appreciate that while her mother was nonresponsive, her mother knew she was there and was listening to every word. The daughter kept shaking her head in disbelief and pushing back, simply unable to believe it was true.

Moments later, the daughter stepped away from the room for a few minutes, and I decided to do a little test. I moved closer to the head of the bed and leaned toward the patient. Remembering the patient was Roman

Catholic, I prayed one of my favorite prayers, saying aloud, "Hail Mary, full of grace. The Lord is with thee. Blessed art thou amongst women, and . . . " As I was praying, I was also watching the patient for any sign of awareness. I learned early on as a new chaplain to be reverent during a prayer but to also watch those I was praying for and with. As I watched the patient, I noticed her toe began to move along in time with the rhythm of my words. So I continued, " . . . blessed is the fruit of thy womb, Jesus. Holy Mary, Mother of God . . . " Sure enough, there was her toe going "tap, tap, tap," keeping the rhythm of my prayer.

I hadn't finished the prayer when the daughter came back into the room. As she approached the bed, I motioned to her and simply pointed to the end of the bed. When I finished the prayer I said it was time for me to go, but I would come back later to check on them. Before I left, I guided her to one side of the bed and told her to place a hand on her mother's shoulder and I would do the same on the other side. I let her know I would lead us in the "Hail Mary" and "Our Father" prayers, and she was welcome to pray aloud with me. I also suggested she should keep her eyes open as we prayed aloud together. I started and she joined in as we prayed together, "Hail Mary, full of grace . . . " and sure enough, the patient's toe began to move and kept pace once again with the words of our prayers. We could hardly finish the prayer, for the daughter began laughing in joyful astonishment. Her prayers were answered. Her mother could hear her and was saying the prayer with her! It was the sign the daughter had been seeking. Her mother found a way to show she was hearing everything and was indeed present with us.

The daughter leaned over her mother in a close embrace, crying and saying, "You are hearing everything, and I know you are, and I love you." She went on to tell her mom they would all be okay and thanked her for letting her know she heard her. It was a wonderful moment! The patient showed her daughter she could hear, knew she was loved, and was not in any pain. We finished our prayers and had a wonderful laugh together before I left.

While this story was a beautiful gift between a mother and daughter, there are times when love is not the first emotion felt at the bedside. Sometimes, families have guilt, anger, even fear. Normally it is my feeling that the bedside of the dying is not a time to air dirty laundry or negative feelings. But there are times when the chaplain does need to step in and be a facilitator. I am ordained as a deacon. The deacon in the Episcopal

Church is called to be a facilitator of lay ministry. I see myself as a facilitator of lay ministry to more than Episcopalians. I minister to families of all faiths, beliefs, and religions. Sometimes these moments call for a child that has not been around much to say or ask their parent for forgiveness. Other times, there may be a family rift, and I can encourage family members to ask for forgiveness and to express their feelings of love. I remind them their loved one can hear and they are with us even if they do not show a response. As a chaplain I have learned to "read the room" quickly to sense the emotions of the room. We can then work with these emotions to facilitate, guide, and walk alongside the patient and their loved ones. It is so important to simply *be* with your loved ones. In our world of email, text, and cell phones we want answers, *now*! It is hard for many of us to just be quiet and still our spirits. Before you air the pain of the past, take a deep breath and just be. Ask, "Is this sharing necessary and, if so, who is it for?" Ask yourself, "Will my sharing of pain make a big difference in eternity?" If it will, then play it through in your mind before you share. Practice. Weigh your words. Pain of the past can be shared with love. Maybe ask for forgiveness if needed, share with the loved one they are forgiven, but, if possible, wrap your words with a shared happy moment you will treasure. Please remember you are together, they are with you, and you are with them, even if the one dying doesn't show physical signs in ways you expect. Your presence is what is most important!

—— *Chapter 28* ——

Spiritual Peace of Mind

GEORGE WAS A PATIENT in a long-term care facility. He had been there long enough that his single room was full of interesting "stuff" he had asked his daughter Sheila to bring from home. Sheila was also her father's durable power of attorney; she tended to his affairs and was attentive to his needs. Mom had been gone a long time, and Dad was now in his late nineties. George also had sons and daughters who lived out of town that he had not heard much from in years. But when the children heard their father wasn't doing well and hospice had been brought in, they suddenly appeared. George had just been told by the cardiologist that his heart could stop at any time and that that was the reason he was a hospice patient.

George had lived on a farm in a lovely home full of antiques he had collected over his lifetime. One of his daughters arrived on a weekend, and no one knew she was in town. She had arrived with a large trailer. It was later assumed she went to the farmhouse, picked the lock, and made herself comfortable there without permission. When she finally came to visit her father, she shared that she had come with a large trailer so that, after her father passed away, she could take the antiques home with her. It was a bizarre interaction. That daughter did not seem to have any manners or sense of decorum. She was very matter of fact; her dad was dying and that meant she could take all his stuff. She had not seen her father in ten years, and I just could not believe her behavior. It was hard to watch, but the chaplain's job was not to get involved.

George was really very easy with his children. One of the things George and I had talked about was that he did not mind that his children were focused on his possessions. For him, if those items meant he got to see his children, then that was okay. George focused on getting his children together for a special evening. As staff, we helped get the children to the facility and helped George plan an evening for them as a family. George told them he wanted to treat everyone to a steak dinner. He used to drive into town every other week for a steak. He loved a specific restaurant, and he really wanted to get his family all around the dinner table one more time. He could not cook like he used to so this would be a way to have a family meal. We helped make reservations, which included his children and their spouses. The aide got George showered, shaved, and dressed. The aide really trimmed him up! He looked so handsome. I was there as the family got ready to leave. It was before 5 p.m. and they had a 6 p.m. reservation. They had enough time to get there along the busy traffic into the city. George and I had planned that I would come back on Monday, and he would share with me the entire family dinner story.

The following Monday, late in the day, I visited George and heard all about his Friday evening. He said it was a wonderful dinner and they had a great visit. He was not a deeply religious man, but he was a spiritual man. He seemed to be genuinely happy about the family dinner. It seemed that on a spiritual level he felt connected once again to his children, and his family sharing that meal together, in a special way, brought him peace. He even said that each of his children had come by earlier that day to see him and say thank you. It turns out that during dinner on Friday night, he told them he wanted each of them to go to his home and walk around to decide what it was that they each wanted. George said his only requirement was he wanted to know what each of his children had selected. He was thankful for the time together and grateful for their visits earlier in the day. It was a joy to see him at peace and to hear about his family being together again.

Early in the morning the next day I got a phone call from the night nurse. She had gone to his room, and he had died. What George had done was get his children together for a wonderful family evening. The evening provided him with some closure with each of his children. It was the last step to getting all his affairs in order. That evening they all learned the farm would be sold and they would each get a share.

While they did not pray together or read from the Bible and do "religious things," there was still something spiritual about their visit. They shared stories, they enjoyed a nice meal together, and they talked about what was important to them. This time together brought out the best in each of them, and their father was able to experience that one last time. There was nothing left to do. His spiritual ducks were all in a row and he was at peace. In less than forty-eight hours after the family dinner, George passed peacefully in his sleep.

The funeral was at his daughter's church in her town nearby. I was asked to do the homily, or short sermon. The pastor did the service, and I did the preaching. I met with the family before the service and asked if it was all right if I said their father did not really beat down the doors of the church. They said yes, that would be okay. They acknowledged their dad was not a churchgoer, but it was important to be in his daughter's church for his funeral. Instead of sitting in the church pews, George helped his friends. George lived the love that Jesus Christ called us to live. He may not have been in the church, but George knew about the love we were to share with each other and do for each other. George helped a lot of people with financial support when they were down and out. I suspect he probably took some friends from his little town and treated them to dinner from time to time at one of his favorite steak houses. Those gathered in the church for his funeral knew George well and loved him dearly. It was a great reminder that you don't have to go every Sunday to a "mid-America God box" to live out Christ's love.

—— *Chapter 29* ——

Yes, They Can Hear Us

I HAD AN AMAZING experience while holding vigil with the family of a dying patient. It never ceases to amaze me how many lessons there are to learn. This particular patient confirmed a belief I have always held about the dying. Further, this death is an example of hospice staff becoming midwives to the spirit.

I was with the patient's daughter and granddaughter. The patient had been nonresponsive and had not eaten or had any liquid for at least twenty-four to thirty-six hours. This was a sign of the dying process, so her family stayed close. Many families are not sure what to do, and they are nervous.

For this patient we witnessed together her anointing led by the priest from the daughter's home parish. Anointing is a very important Catholic sacrament giving the patient, alert or not, the forgiveness of all sins with blessed oil and sign of the cross. I always want to give the family an opportunity to be present for the anointing and do my best to coordinate with the priest and the family to allow this time to happen when they are together.

Next, as we sat beside the patient's bed, I did with them what I do with many patients' families. I ask them to tell me stories about their loved one and to share their fond memories as a family. I have always marveled how quickly, when stories are shared, all the tension eases and a peace resonates in the room. The daughter and granddaughter immediately started telling stories and their favorite moments. One of the favorites that I still remember is the lesson bestowed to the granddaughter on the day of her First

Communion. She dressed in a beautiful white dress paired with brand new black patent Mary Janes complete with white socks trimmed in lace. She was dressed just perfectly for the occasion and was beaming with delight. It was raining outside so, from the safety of the garage, she climbed into the car with her parents and grandparents and started for the church.

They were running a little late as they arrived, so her dad pulled the car close to the door where the children were going in and let her out of the car. Just as soon as the car door closed behind her, she slipped into a puddle of water and her perfect little outfit was drenched! She burst into tears and wailed for help as Grandma quickly got out of the car. Grandma reached down and grabbed her little hand, lifting her from the ground, and swiftly walked her into the church. They went into the restroom and Grandma got her all cleaned up. Before leaving the restroom, she knelt and said to her granddaughter, "You are the only one that knows your clothes are wet and they will soon dry. What you are going to do now is go out there and smile. If anyone notices, you keep your smile, nod, and say, 'Thank you, I am aware,' and gracefully move on." What a great lesson in confidence and perseverance when things do not go as planned!

They continued with stories of Easter egg hunts where they haphazardly discovered one of the eggs wasn't cooked and another was left forgotten until a mysterious smell began to rise from its hiding place. There were stories of school events, family gatherings, and their favorite meals from the woman who hated to cook. It was a wonderful experience and allowed them both to laugh, cry, and reminisce about the lifetime they shared with their beloved mother and grandmother as she slept quietly beside them.

After some time, I excused myself from the room to check in with the hospice staff and to coordinate logistics. I really wanted to stay with the family, as I had gotten to know them and had grown close with the patient and her family. With the details sorted, I let the staff know I could stay through the rest of my shift and returned to the patient's room. When I walked back into the room, the family was very quiet. I turned to the patient and noticed her breathing had changed a little bit and was deeper and slower than before. She did not seem to be in any pain, so I sat back down next to the family. It was obvious to me that the daughter and granddaughter had been talking while I was out of the room, and something was on their minds. The granddaughter broke their silence, turning to me to ask if her grandmother could hear them talking, inquiring if it was possible that she could hear their stories and was aware of their presence there with her.

Since her grandmother had not been responsive, it was a great question and one that I am asked often. I let her know that yes, absolutely I believed she could hear them and knew they were present. As a hospice chaplain we all believe one of the last things we lose as we are dying is our hearing and sense of presence of others around us. Just as I had paused to take a breath, the patient suddenly responded on her own to her granddaughter's question, saying, "Yes." Her voice was as clear as the conversation I was having with her family. She said nothing more. Her eyes did not open, nor did her body move. She simply said, "Yes," affirming to her family she was listening and was feeling the love they were sharing. She had put the exclamation point on what I had just shared. Daughter and granddaughter were shocked and amazed at her response. They both felt they had received a special gift in knowing she knew how much she was loved and cherished by them. Their hearts were full, knowing she could feel their love and knew they were there with her.

She died soon after, with daughter and granddaughter holding her hands, telling her how much she was loved. Knowing she could hear them, their words flowed with ease. They shared how much they would miss her and how her life had impacted theirs and how she would forever be in their hearts. It was a holy, peaceful death. I later had the opportunity to officiate at the memorial service as a celebration of her life.

One of the things I asked was if I could share in my homily the experience of her saying, "Yes" and the impact it had on them as a family. I shared how important it is to gather as a family and tell stories around your dying loved ones. Laugh with one another, cry with one another, and share the love that you have experienced as a family, knowing in your heart that your loved one is listening and they are there with you enjoying and reliving the memories alongside you. Even if they don't respond, know they are with you, and you are with them. Share how much they are loved and will be missed. Share how they will live forever in your hearts.

— Chapter 30 —

Comfort in Prayer

It was a Sunday morning, and I was the hospice chaplain on call. My husband and I were heading to church, and we took two cars. We learned early on when I was on call to always be prepared. It had been proven that if we took only one car, I would absolutely get a call. If we took two cars, it was less likely.

Well, on this day, even with two cars, I got a call right as we pulled into the church parking lot. The call was for a man north of the city who was a home patient. It would be a journey to get to him, so I said goodbye to my husband and headed north. When I arrived, I pulled into the driveway of a very large, beautiful home. I followed the long path from the driveway to the front door and rang the bell. I was greeted by a stunningly gorgeous, regal woman. I can still remember she wore a loose white linen top with matching pants that made her dark hair, soft facial features, and natural beauty shine bright. She was simply radiant. Her clothes and overall appearance struck me as unusually formal for an early Sunday morning vigil with a dying husband. She introduced herself as Ophelia and said she would take me to see the patient. As we entered the bedroom where he was, she introduced me as the chaplain to the gentleman, but she didn't stay. The room was so very quiet. The patient was lying in the bed, clearly weak but alert, and he greeted me very kindly. He said he appreciated that I came, but he did not need a chaplain. I let him know that was fine but that I would be there a little while and I would check out with him before I left. He agreed that would be okay and I left the room, softly closing the door behind me. Not every visit needs a prayer. Sometimes it's just important you were there.

I returned to the large, open living area and found Ophelia sitting quietly. I sat down across from her and started a conversation. It became clear they were a couple, and she was struggling as she grieved his death. I learned the patient was keeping her at a distance and was not allowing her to care for him. That explained why she had left the room so quickly and maybe why she had been so quiet. He wasn't allowing himself to be vulnerable even in death. He was trying to be strong and perhaps felt expressing no emotion and keeping her at a distance was helping them both. But it was clear Ophelia desperately wanted to be with him. She shared how she wanted to hold his hand and to just be in the room with him. Ophelia really needed something to comfort her, since the patient was not allowing her to comfort him.

As we spoke, I said I had something in my car that might help her feel some comfort. She accepted my offer, so I went to my car. I had just received a small bag of prayer beads from my church, and this was the first time I would share them with a patient or their loved one. Without looking into the bag, I grabbed a set of beads and went back inside the home. When I reached out my hand to pass the beads to Ophelia, we both laid eyes on the most magnificent turquoise beads! Each bead gleamed with a deep, rich turquoise color that was as regal and stunning as Ophelia. It was clear God intended these beads for her. I shared with her the design and structure of the prayer beads. Then, I gave her several ideas about how she could use them in prayer or simply hold them in her hands for comfort.

We talked for a little while longer and then it was time for me to leave. I asked Ophelia if it would be okay for me to say goodbye to her partner before leaving. She nodded her approval and said she would stay in the living room, and I could visit with him alone. I knocked on the bedroom door and slowly entered and let him know I was leaving. I can't tell you why, but I just knew the patient did not need me to offer to pray. We spoke for a few minutes, and he said there was nothing more he needed. I began for the door while thinking how the patient was still stoically facing his death. As I started to open the bedroom door, he asked if I could say a prayer before leaving. I asked him if he wanted Ophelia to join us. He said no. I stood next to his bed. I said a heart prayer and the Lord's Prayer. I invited him to join if he wished. After closing, I excused myself from the bedroom and headed back to the front of the home. There was Ophelia, snuggled into a window seat in front of a very large picture window overlooking their backyard. She had her head bowed and eyes closed in prayer with the turquoise beads. I thanked God in that moment for bringing her comfort through those beads and quietly said goodbye as I stepped out the front door. I left hoping their home was more at peace than it was when I arrived. I marveled again at the silence coming from their home.

In the bag I was carrying, there were at least fifteen different sets of prayer beads. There were beads of all colors and styles. After that visit, it became very clear to me that God had a plan for each set of prayer beads. God placed the beads he designed for Ophelia into my hand that day. Seeing her in the window seat praying with those beads held tightly in her hands, I felt those beads would be with her for a very long time. Yes, they were meant to be hers and they seemed to bring her peace and comfort in a time when she needed it most.

Two wonderful ladies from my parish first introduced me to Anglican prayer beads. They were making them by hand as they prayed, told stories, and laughed over them. The priest had blessed all the prayer beads together, sending them to go out into the world with me as their carrier.

—— *Chapter 31* ——

Let Me into Heaven

I WAS THE CHAPLAIN with a hospice program when I met a dear patient, Marybeth. Our office got a call late one afternoon with an interview request from a family who was admitting a loved one at an area hospital. They were interested in hospice care and were interviewing several programs to find the best fit for their loved one. I was the chaplain on call that day, so I went to meet the family, introduce myself, and share what our hospice program had to offer. Each hospice has its own personality, so it's important to talk to the family about what hospice is and is not, as well as to give them a feel for what our hospice experience would be like.

I had my business cards and brochures in hand when I knocked on Marybeth's door. I was admitted by three members of Marybeth's family: her husband, daughter, and son. As I walked into the room, I noticed Marybeth was in the bed with the covers pulled all the way up to her chin, looking very much asleep or maybe even comatose. She gave no sign she would be part of the conversation. I asked the family if they wanted to stay in the patient's room or to go sit in the lounge to talk. The family said they wanted to do the interview there in the room and invited me to take a seat beside the bed.

They were kind and gracious as they introduced themselves and shared some details about their wife and mother. I told them about our hospice and the care team members that were involved. I explained the roles of each team member as well as what the family could expect from our hospice team, especially when the dying process started. I emphasized there was one part of our program that made us unique. During the dying process, at least one member of the team was present with them twenty-four hours a day. I told them it is usually the chaplain or the social worker during the day and a nurse at night who would be there the most. After the patient had passed, there would be a bereavement coordinator who would stay in contact for a year. I went on to share that we believed holding vigil was one of the most precious things we could do for our patients and their families. It was important to us that they were never alone, and we would be there to support the patient's spirit and the family.

They immediately asked why they had to have a chaplain. Marybeth's husband shared that he was Roman Catholic, but Marybeth was a non-believer and would not need a chaplain. They were worried the chaplain would try to convert her or force a religious tradition on her. I shared that they did not have to have the chaplain. And that the chaplain may come to visit but would visit only with the intention of walking gently behind to support Marybeth's spirit and the family.

We talked for quite a while, discussing many questions. We went on to talk about the stages of the dying process and what happens at the time of death. I walked them through all the details and exactly how we stay with the family until the undertaker arrives. If someone passes away and we are not there, a member of the team will come as soon as possible so that the family is not alone. I also conveyed how our team directs everything that happens after death, coordinating the details according to their wishes and supporting them along the way.

Throughout the interview there was no sign that Marybeth heard anything. Her eyes were still closed; she had not stirred in the bed or made any noise. As we closed the conversation, I made a big effort to reinforce the role of the chaplain. I said again that the chaplain was not there to convert and was there to support them and their needs. We closed our conversation and they thanked me for my time. I really appreciated how interested they were in learning as much as they could about our program. They were clearly devoted to finding the best fit to support Marybeth.

The next day the family called to say they had completed their interviews with several hospices and had chosen ours. I was thrilled to hear the news. Before getting started, though, there was a question about a chaplain. Would it be okay for the chaplain to visit in the next couple of days? They accepted our offer, and I was delighted to go back to the hospital a few days later to make my first hospice visit with Marybeth.

When I got to Marybeth's room, I was surprised to see her sitting up, wide awake on the sofa. Her presence was completely different from what I expected based on her condition the day I interviewed with the family. I introduced myself and we went on to have a lovely conversation about a lot of different things. We talked a little about religion in our first visit, but I was not going to press the topic. She did share that she did not go to church with her family but that her children were raised in the Roman Catholic Church. From our conversation, I *suspected* that when she married her husband, she had to commit to raising her children as Roman Catholic, since that was her husband's faith. And I believe that was likely very hard for her, but she did not say that out loud.

Shortly after our first visit, I was told by the nurse manager that Marybeth enjoyed my visit but did not need my services anymore. As a program we acknowledged her wishes and reminded her that if she ever did need a chaplain, we were a phone call away. About six weeks went by before we got a call from the family requesting a visit from the chaplain. Specifically, they asked for the "woman chaplain" who had met with them before.

I went to visit Marybeth, and the first thing she wanted to know was how long my visits would last. I told her my visits would last as long as they needed to. After a moment, she nodded "okay" and asked me what I wanted to talk about. I let her know that the chaplain does not come to talk about what they want to talk about. I was there to listen to what she wanted to talk about. To ease into it, I asked her to tell me about herself. She started with her family and then shared how much she loved her job managing a doctor's office. She started to laugh when she remembered how sometimes she needed to make two sandwiches for lunch because the doctor admired her sandwiches so much that she would give hers to him. She got so tired of going hungry, she started to make two. One of the doctor's favorites was a cold meatloaf sandwich. That was my favorite too! It is hard to beat a cold meatloaf sandwich on super soft, spongy bread with Miracle Whip! We laughed together, agreeing it was the only way to eat meatloaf. It was wonderful to find something we had in common, and from that moment on I got to be a weekly visitor. Over many visits we enjoyed conversations about weeding the garden, our children and how we raised them, meals we cooked, books we read, and activities with our families. During one visit, I did have the courage to ask her what she did while her family went to church. She said she was able to have cherished alone time and enjoyed gardening in the spring and summer and reading in the fall and winter. She used the time to do the things that gave her joy. I did not ask any more questions about church, and I never asked her if she wanted to pray. I always felt that if she wanted to pray, she would let me know.

And one day it did happen. We were sitting together talking when she suddenly stopped the conversation to ask me if I would pray that God would let her into his heaven. I let her know that we could pray right then and there, but she said she did not know how to pray. I told her that prayer was simply a conversation with God. And that God pretty much knows what we are going to say before we say it, but we say it anyway. And sometimes prayer is merely being quiet and still.

We ended that visit with a prayer, and when I came back the next time, she said she was still struggling with how to pray. I let her know sometimes we need something to help us know when to be quiet and still and shared how I use prayer beads as a tool to help me pray. I did not tell her they were Anglican or Episcopal prayer beads. I also did not refer to them as a rosary even though prayer beads are very similar. I explained that prayer beads have been used for well over two thousand years by many religions as people traveled throughout the world. I let her know I would be happy to share a set with her if she was interested but would have to go to my car to get them. I do not want to ever presume that patients want or need prayer beads, and I do not ever want to "sell" patients on the beads, so I never carry them with me.

I went to my car to get a set and returned. I remember thinking the beads were very beautiful as she took them and held them tightly. From then on, each week she would tell me how she had used her prayer beads for praying. I told her that the more she used them, the more her body would respond and relax, knowing it was time to pray. And over time, it would become like holding God's hand. She agreed.

Marybeth passed away when I wasn't on call, but I was asked to do her service. I met with the family and told them it would be a traditional Episcopal service and laid out how it would be very similar to the Roman Catholic service. They agreed with the service plans but said they had one big question. They wanted to know if Marybeth could be buried with her prayer beads. I told them that would be their choice.

It was a wonderful service and, when it came time to place her coffin in the vault, I knew God had Marybeth well in hand, so my ministry then was really to her family. As I moved with my blessed oils to make the sign of the cross, I turned to her family to share that I thought it would be okay with Marybeth if we sent her off with the "Hail Mary" and "Our Father" prayers. They were very eager, so when I started the "Hail Mary," I let my voice fade, allowing the family's voices to take over, carrying the prayer forward with their voices instead of the chaplain's, as they prayed for their beloved mother and wife. Following the prayers everyone placed a flower in Marybeth's coffin. The family shared Marybeth was buried with her prayer beads in her hands.

I did not hear from Marybeth's family after the service. After a patient passes, I hand off all my families to the bereavement coordinator for the next phase. And when I finish a funeral, I hug the family as my final good-bye. I had the privilege of time with Marybeth. I also had the privilege of walking with someone who found God. It was an amazing gift! As chaplain, I give my patients to God and hold on to the memories. One of the things I was reminded of during my time with Marybeth was that God comes when God comes. A person finds God when they find God. I am simply there as a gentle reminder of his presence in the world. God does the rest.

I will never forget her request of "Will you pray that your God will let me into his heaven?" As I told Marybeth, I also tell you. We are all welcome in heaven and God wants each of us to be there with him.

—— *Chapter 32* ——

We Want Beads Too

I REMEMBER THIS VISIT as though it was yesterday. I was covering for another chaplain when I found myself in the inner city, visiting a dying patient I had never met. I was greeted by a woman who said she was the patient's daughter. She described her father, Orville, as a loving, warm father and grandfather and told me the family was surrounding him. She introduced me to Orville and then to other members of the family. I asked for a chair so I could sit by the patient on his level. Also, I asked the family if we (the patient and I) could talk a little while privately. It is unusual for a dying patient to be so alert, and I needed to know without distraction and embarrassment for the patient how he was *really* doing.

As we talked, he told me he was having a hard time praying. We chatted about different methods for prayer, and I shared with him about using prayer beads and how sometimes the prayer beads are a tool to help us focus. I shared the history of prayer beads and that the beads I share with patients are made by the ladies of my church and blessed by our priest. No two sets are alike. Orville took great interest in the idea of the beads, so I offered to go to my car and bring back a set of prayer beads for him.

As I left the home and walked to my car parked in front, I noticed two very tall, very large men dressed all in black leather walking toward me. Yes, I could have let myself feel intimidated by their ominous presence. They felt entirely out of place in this neighborhood. I looked around, wondering where they had come from, and prayed that they would keep on walking and pass me by. In a loud, deep voice, one of the men asked what I was doing there. I froze in place, praying silently, "Be still my spirit" while simultaneously begging my legs to not shake. Speaking as confidently as I could, I told them I was retrieving a set of prayer beads for a dying patient. The same man quickly retorted they wanted prayer beads too. I was taken aback by their hasty demand because prayer beads were not casual commodities, and I did not give them out casually but rather for God's purposes.

With strength from the Holy Spirit, I let them know they could have their own prayer beads, but they would have to wait because I needed to go back inside to be with a patient and his family. They nodded and agreed to wait by my car until I returned. Relieved, I reached into my bag and grabbed a set of beads for Orville. Tightly clutching the beads in one hand, I closed and locked the car door with the other. I prayed silently as I walked away from the men, asking God to please find another place for these intimidating men to be before I returned.

When I got back to Orville's room, I opened my hand to give Orville the prayer beads. This was the first time I had seen the beads, because I had just stuck my hand in the bag and grabbed a set of beads. Orville and I saw the beads at the same time. I couldn't believe my eyes. The beads were tiger eye beads. I had never seen a set like these before and I have never been given a set like these since. I thought I had seen all the beads, but I must have missed these. How could I have missed such a distinctive set? The beads were perfect for Orville. This sweet man of African descent received the tiger eye beads with a big smile. I explained to him I don't go through and select the beads; I just grab a set and hope they are just right for the patient.

The visit closed with everyone gathered around the bed, holding hands. I said a heart prayer and one of the sons added his own prayer. We all said the Lord's Prayer together and closed with a rousing rendition of "Amazing Grace."

As it turned out, the men outside waited! About forty-five minutes to an hour later, I came out of the house and returned to my car and there they were; the two men had patiently waited for me. I again opened the side door of my car and reached into my bag to grab a set of beads for each of them. Just as quickly as they had first appeared, they took their beads and moved on down the street. They never said another word to me but simply walked away. Ever since then, I have always wondered if those two men were angels. I never choose the beads for the person; God chooses. Often a patient or family member will ask me if I selected the color or style of beads just for them. In the case of the dying man on this day, I pulled a beautiful set of tiger eye beads from my bag. I knew immediately they were perfect for him, and his family agreed. It may be that God sent those men for a purpose. Maybe God was challenging me and my promise to share the beads with anyone who asks. I truly believe angels are among us, but they don't wear signs. I was truly out of my comfort zone in that area of the city, and God was reminding me to trust in him and the Holy Spirit.

Chapter 33

Death Is Not Always Peaceful

Part 1

IT IS IMPORTANT TO share with you that not every death is peaceful or beautiful. I was the chaplain at a long-term care facility and like most facilities we had patients who were also hospice patients. I made a small paper dove about the size of an old half-dollar coin. The dove would go on the nameplate outside the patient's room to let the staff know this patient was a hospice patient. We all would be more attuned to the needs and circumstances that might be unique to a hospice patient. This also let the communion ministers know they were taking communion to a hospice patient. In turn, the communion ministers would share with me any change in the patient's condition.

One of the hospice patients was Elizabeth. She was in her seventies and she was a long-time alcohol abuser. Her children told me that their mom had end-stage liver disease. Her husband had died many years ago. Her children had brought a few things from home but not a lot. She had pictures, but nothing warm and personal. Elizabeth's children had tried, but the room was still a sterile room. The children didn't visit often and, when they did, they did not stay long. The children were showing us, the facility staff, that they didn't have a warm relationship with Mom.

When Elizabeth's body entered the dying process, the hospice staff called her children. The children came to be there but spent most of their time in the hallway instead of in the room with their mother. When Elizabeth entered the final stages, she was no longer agitated and she was no longer responsive. I stood out in the hall with Elizabeth's children a lot for those few days. They shared a lot about their mom and growing up. They said Dad had been a very successful investor and their mom was a "homemaker." Mom and Dad had an agreement that Mom would always be ready to entertain Dad's clients at a moment's notice in their beautiful home. The kids talked about how there was always someone coming for dinner, so the kids were often eating in the kitchen by themselves. The family rarely ate meals together because, when they weren't entertaining, Mom and Dad would go out. Neither Mom nor Dad would go to any of the kids' activities because they usually occurred during the best time to meet clients. As soon as the children had their own drivers' licenses, the kids got cars so they could get themselves where they needed to go, and Mom did not have to worry about that anymore. Mom dressed them perfectly for outings and church each week. From the outside looking in, they were a gorgeous family who had it all. Mom and children attended church every week. Dad went to church on Christmas and Easter. Elizabeth was always more concerned about what she was wearing than the theology. The feeling was that Mom and Dad spent more time at the club and having parties than time spent expressing their love to the kids. Her adult children shared how their growing up was a pattern of parenting that they weren't following with their own children.

Elizabeth died with only the facility staff present. I did not follow up with her children after they left. I can still see them standing outside Elizabeth's room, a distance away from their mother as she was dying. By the time she got to our facility, the alcohol had taken her liver and her mind. I never had a chance to have a conversation with her. She might have been the perfect wife, but she was not a perfect mother. This was not a beautiful nor peaceful death.

Part 2

I had been visiting a man in his home every two weeks for a good three months. Larry was very involved in his congregation. I learned over many visits that he was the guy who was always there for church events, was the Boy Scout leader, and I suspect was viewed as the model family man in the community. He and his wife had several children. They had moved from a large house to a small apartment once the children were grown, but the kids were frequently there. It was not a joyous house; it was a *busy* house where someone was constantly coming and going. With each visit, they were so busy "doing" that I often wondered what was wrong.

Larry had a bed in the living room. He had trouble breathing, so for many of my visits he would be sitting next to the bed in an upright wooden chair. I was called when he was dying. I arrived, and he was sitting upright in the chair instead of lying in the bed. He was really laboring to breathe. His oxygen machine was loud. Everyone was quiet, but the children were in and out of the room, boys over there, girls over here, and then outside and inside. It was constant movement. But nobody ever came near Larry. They just stayed in their little groups. Larry's wife always escaped to the kitchen when I arrived.

Larry was agitated. I asked him what was wrong, and he said he was worried about dying. But talking was too difficult. I asked if I could pray, and he said, "Please." I said a heart prayer, trying to help him relax, but nothing was helping. There was no singing, no talking, no praying that would help the man relax. It is important to help the dying be calm and relaxed so they can let go. Larry held on to the arms of the chair with white knuckles and remained very rigid and tense. He would not take any pain medicine from the nurse. He said he wanted to stay alert. I think Larry thought if he stayed alert, he would not die. As a chaplain I could almost feel the negative vibes around him. It reminded me of an old movie where these little black things come out of the ground to take the evil character away. It still gives me chills thinking about it.

I left Larry in the living room with the nurse while I spent some time with the daughters in the kitchen. I listened to them talk about their father, and something unspoken was there, but it was not coming out. They just kept saying he would be at peace soon, and it would all be over once their father had died. We had visited for a while when one daughter finally alluded to something sexual that connected Dad and the girls. It was not my role to ask questions or to probe. I was there to support Larry and his family.

Later I was back in the living room and no one else was around. I took the opportunity to ask him if there was anything that he needed to tell the pastor. Should I call the pastor? I reminded him that the pastor had prayed with him, but I knew he would come back. Larry insisted there was nothing he needed to talk to the pastor about. Larry said he was afraid the pastor would not allow him to have a funeral in the church. I told Larry God would forgive him for any sins, but he said God would not forgive him. I shared there is nothing that God won't forgive; all we have to do is ask to be forgiven. But that was it—at that moment he threw his head back, eyes wide open and he was gone. As soon as the nurse said it out loud, the entire family was immediately in the room, including Mom standing next to him. It was like they all had to see it for themselves to know Dad/Larry was gone.

Maybe saying those words out loud was enough to allow him to let go, but it was a horrible death. He was sitting upright and rigidly in that chair, holding on so tight his knuckles were white. He fought so hard thinking if he stayed alert and awake, he could stave off death. Death comes when death comes. God comes when God comes. We have an illusion that we can control God, but we are not in control. God is.

Part 3

I was called to see a woman living in an assisted living center. Her death was the second death I ever experienced where the patient was alert until the last second. The nurse and I were the only people in the room with her. Her family had come to see her a few days prior, and it was obvious they were coming to say goodbye out of duty, not love. The patient stated early on as I visited her weekly how she had had a life her family had not agreed with. "But I had fun!" she shared. She had lived all over, and she knew powerful men. The facility staff appeared to know her, and they didn't appear to like her—but no one said why. As she was dying, the hospice nurse and I were the only ones caring for her.

The hospice nurse and I were holding the patient as she was dying. The nurse was on one side of the bed, and I was on the other side. I had to push the bed out slightly from the wall so I could get to her other side. She was yelling in anger, not in pain, and she wanted to sit up. She kept reaching out to grab a hand to help her out of the bed. Her legs were moving, and her arms were flailing about. It took everything we had to hold on to her and keep her in the bed. I believe she was trying to run from death. It seemed she felt that if she moved fast enough, she could get away from death.

As she died, the nurse and I felt evil in some form came to get her. Her sin was heavy, but we never knew what her sins were. Darkness filled the room and it was a horrible death. I worked with the nurse for many years after that, and, on her final day, she came to me and asked if I remembered that death—it remained with us both and we agreed the memory would never leave us.

Chapter 34

Taking Jesus into Your Heart

WHEN YOU WORK FOR a regional hospice program, inevitably you will have patients from the surrounding metro area to serve. As chaplain, I took rotations for the on-call schedule in addition to the clinical staff. Each time I was on call, I would carefully lay out my clothes, shoes, and purse near the door so I would be ready in a moment's notice to go anywhere across the city. One day, I got a call at 4:45 a.m. for a patient that lived in a long-term care facility over forty-five minutes away in an area I did not normally cover. I immediately dressed, oriented myself on the directions (this was before GPS), and set out for what felt like a long drive in the dawn hours.

The family of this patient had called requesting a chaplain. One of the patient's daughters met me at the facility door and appeared very anxious. She pleaded for help, saying, "Daddy has never said he has taken Jesus into his heart, and we really need Daddy to say that. We need you to get him to say that." I listened and reminded myself that I support the patient and their family.

I followed the daughter down the hall and into the patient's room where we were met by a second daughter. His bed was on the floor. This is a common practice for hospice patients who have falls. I knelt at his side and introduced myself as the chaplain. I then sat down on the floor, crossing my legs. The daughters stayed in the room but quietly stood along the wall, watching us and listening. I turned to the patient and asked if I could hold his hand. He nodded as he reached out and gave me his hand.

Often when I am with a dying patient, I will offer to pray or sing to them. I gently held his hand and asked if I could sing a hymn to him. He nodded yes. I had a song in mind but first asked if he would be offended if I sang a children's hymn. He said that would be okay, so I began to sing "Jesus Loves Me." He quietly sang the verses with me as I continued to hold his hand. Following the hymn, I asked if we could pray the Lord's Prayer and he said most of the prayer with me. We had a quiet conversation. Then before leaving, I asked him if I could do a closing prayer and what he wanted me to pray for. I asked him if he knew God loved him and he said yes. He said he wanted to pray that he would go to heaven. I led all of us in prayer, and he thanked me kindly as I stood to leave.

The daughters followed me out of the room but were not happy. They indicated that I had not met their expectations. They insisted that their Dad had not declared that "he had taken Jesus into his heart." They were telling me that I needed to get him to say the exact words like in the Bible out loud so they could hear it. I told them that he had just sung "Jesus Loves Me"; wasn't that enough? By singing along he showed that he knew Jesus loved him and he loved Jesus. But they still disagreed. The older daughter pleaded, "Pastor says you have to say you have taken Jesus in your heart to go to heaven. Daddy will not go to heaven unless he says it!" I said I was sorry and repeated that their dad did have Jesus in his heart. Dissatisfied, they thanked me anyway for coming, and I left.

I went to the nurse's station to check out before going home. From the station I could see that the daughters had moved their dying father into a wheelchair and taken him outside onto the patio. They were pleading and begging him to say he was taking Jesus into his heart over and over. Nowhere in the Bible does it say you have to do this. Nor is it required to announce it for others to hear. Your heart connects with Jesus and that is enough. These women did not get it and they probably never would. The Lord's Prayer and singing "Jesus loves Me" was still not enough to meet their definition of being "saved."

The chaplain is never there to convert anyone and accepts where the patient is theologically. I was not there to fix anything or to change anyone. I was there to support this dying man. I was not there to do what the daughters wanted me to do. I was there to walk with that man and meet him where he was. It was also not my role to coach or scold those daughters. I felt sorry for that man and his daughters. I took my frustration to the road and tried not to play angry bumper cars on my long drive home. I shared my thoughts with God, and I prayed for that gentleman and his daughters. Jesus was already in his heart; this I know. A chaplain visits to be present and support and *never* to evangelize or convert a patient or family.

Chapter 35

A Very Human Story

I WAS MAKING MY first visit to a hospice patient in a long-term care facility. Before meeting Millie, I learned she was in the facility because it was hard for her husband in his late eighties and their family to care for her at home. Her body was failing from terminal cancer, but, mentally, she was still strong. She had her own single room that her family had decorated beautifully. It looked like a bedroom rather than the room of a patient in a care facility. They had framed family photos on the walls, trinkets, and precious keepsakes all around on the side tables and her dresser, a pretty bedspread, and matching curtains to make it feel more like home. I really felt like I had stepped into her home. Later I would reflect on how her children had outdone themselves.

When I came to her room, I found the door partially open. I paused to knock and waited for a response. She did not answer so I slowly opened door. She was in bed, eyes closed, appearing to be asleep. I remember that this dear lady looked more like the fairy godmother from Cinderella than a hospice patient. I stepped back into the hallway to talk to the nurse and learned the patient was resting but it would be okay for me to go in. I returned to her room. Slowly and quietly, I pulled a chair close to the head of the bed. As I sat down, I tapped her lightly on the shoulder. She rolled over looking at me with her eyes still closed, and softly said, "Not tonight, Honey." The meaning of her words washed over me as I felt a slow smile on my face. Millie slowly opened her eyes and gasped! I could tell she was embarrassed and surprised to see me instead of her husband. I smiled and said it was okay, letting her know I was a wife of over forty years, and I understood "Not tonight, Honey." I introduced myself as the hospice chaplain and let her know I had just come to say hello. She smiled broadly and said, "Thank the Lord you are a woman! I would never be able to talk to a man after greeting you that way." We went on to have a wonderful conversation that day and on many days to come. I listened to her life story over a period of months before she passed. We visited every other week, when she shared with me about her children, her husband, and her strong faith. Millie's family was at her bedside with me and our hospice nurse when she let go and took God's hand. Her death was a quiet gentle passing.

The humanness of being a hospice chaplain is invaluable for connecting to basic human needs. As chaplain you must be prepared for "life's things" and precious moments. Not everything that happens in hospice will be deeply spiritual or have a theological edge to it. But to be able to chuckle with her and have empathy opened a door to a good relationship between chaplain and a patient. If I had acted shocked or allowed myself to be judgmental, there never would have been a relationship. When Millie said, "Not tonight, Honey," my immediate response was to giggle because in my humanness I could relate. It was not my job to shame her or show judgment but to meet her where she was. Millie was so at peace, in a place that felt like home, she responded in love to one she believed was her husband.

Something I so often see forgotten, by children and family members, is making the loved one's long-term space a safe and peaceful place, as close to being like home as possible. Long-term care rooms need to have the personal treasures of home.

One thing we have done many times toward the end is encourage a couple to lie in bed and hold one another. There is something so safe, comforting, and normal that allows the body to relax and let go. This was home where Millie died, in the arms of her husband with her children at the bedside. Millie and her husband had a wonderful relationship and happy marriage. In a loving relationship of any kind, God is present. For me on that day as chaplain, it was about my presence and being open to whatever God presented. And God can surprise you! I was present with Millie reflecting on my life history as a wife, mother, and chaplain. As chaplain, you hope to walk gently behind the patient and their family on this holy and sacred journey. Meeting the patient where they are and with the presence of the Holy Spirit, God opens the door for a spiritual connection.

---- *Chapter 36* ----

My Mom's Story and a Case of Terminal Restlessness

WHEN MY MOM BECAME a hospice patient she wasn't doing well. Her heart was tired. She really wanted to be part of the hospice that I worked for, and we made those arrangements. But I let her know that I would not be her chaplain. Another chaplain would visit her as well as a hospice nurse I knew very well. Mom had a very slow decline.

It was December and Mom's care facility was hosting its annual holiday party. On that Thursday evening, my husband and I went as her guests and had a wonderful time. We returned to her apartment to talk well into the evening. It really was an enjoyable evening. When it was time for us to leave, we wheeled Mom in her wheelchair to the main door to say goodbye and see us go. When we did that, the owner of the facility, who was always very sweet to Mom, said she would wheel her back to her apartment. She stayed with her long after we left and talked with my mom for over an hour. She was just so wonderful to her.

The next morning after the holiday party I got a phone call around 5 a.m. saying that my mom had fallen, and she was being taken to the hospital to be evaluated. I rushed out the door and got to the hospital at the same time as the hospice nurse. We learned Mom had gone to the bathroom and slipped and fallen on her way back to her bed. The staff found her and called for an ambulance but did not call the hospice staff or me as they should have done. We never would have sent her to the hospital. It scared my mom to tears, causing her to be disoriented. It was horrible to see her that way when I got there. When I arrived, Mom was a mess, and it was all totally unnecessary. Between 5 a.m. and 1 p.m. the hospice nurse and I got Mom back to the facility and in her bed. I hired around-the-clock caregivers, so she was not alone again. I called my siblings to share what had happened and to be ready in case things changed.

I waited in my mom's apartment until the first caregiver arrived. Mom was still in bed and settling down. The caregiver that came initially was a lady whom my mom knew. It was nice to have a familiar person there. Mom and her helper were going to look at Christmas decorations in the facility, so I said goodbye as the caregiver helped Mom dress. Later that day around 8 p.m. the next caregiver checked in with me, letting me know she was there and was planning to stay all night and into Saturday. The plan was, for each twelve-hour shift, the caregivers would check in throughout the weekend.

Saturday afternoon I got a call that Mom did not want to go back to her apartment. She just wanted to be pushed around the facility. There were a lot of holiday decorations, and the facility was built around a nice courtyard. They said she did not want to go to bed, she just wanted to be pushed around the facility, seemingly enjoying the company. Well, she was my mom, and I was not paying attention to any of the signs. I was the daughter, not the chaplain, and I missed it. I missed that Mom was dying, because she did not show the typical signs for any of us. The hospice nurses were visiting every eight hours and they did not see any signs of the dying process either, or they would have called me. The reason Mom did not want to return to her room was that she had "terminal restlessness." The hospice nurses checked on Mom every eight hours and they were not seeing any physical signs of dying. A dying person's body usually gives you signs of the dying process. There can be discoloration of the hands, back of the leg, or feet. Breathing can be laboring or challenging. But Mom didn't have any of those signs. Terminal restlessness can be part of the dying process but not all the time.

On Sunday, my phone rang just as we were going into church. The hospice nurse told me I needed to hurry; Mom's condition was changing quickly. My husband and I left immediately. I called my sister and brother to get them on their way. Mom had finally calmed down enough that she would lie down. When I arrived around 10:45 a.m., Mom grabbed my hand

and said, "Oh, Becca, you are here." It was the last she spoke. Mom grabbed my hand and held on tight. The hospice nurse came and stayed with us. My sister and her husband started the six-hour drive to get to us. Meanwhile, our daughters came and sat on the bed talking to "Mimi" like she was wide awake. My brother and his family came, followed by our sons. All realizing that "Yes, Mimi was dying." Over the time from noon to 8:30 in the evening there were children and grandchildren coming in and out, talking to Mom. We all shared stories and told her many times about how she was loved. Even though she never responded verbally, I know she knew we were there. I have suspected many times that the dying think they are talking to us even if we can't hear them. Our priest from the cathedral came and anointed Mom. All those present held hands around her bed and prayed.

My sister and her family finally arrived about 8:30 p.m. Mom's daughters and granddaughters were in the room, sitting on her king-size bed. Mom wasn't verbal, but she would squeeze our hands, letting us know she knew we were there. We sang, we laughed, and we talked for hours. The hospice nurse was magnificent in sitting with us. Just before 11 p.m., the hospice nurse who had been providing medicines to help Mom's comfort said she wanted to check Mom's vital signs. It was then that she let us know Mom was gone. While we talked to her, laughed, and sang, she simply slipped away. It was a truly holy and a sacred transition from one world to the next. I can't imagine any more lovely way to go than to have your children and grandchildren sitting on the large bed with you. It was the kind of death I think everybody would hope for.

When Mom died and the funeral home came, we made sure she was a direct cremation *without embalming*. This is what my mom wanted, so I had bought a special package with a local funeral home for Mom to have direct cremation. It had been at least five years before she died, and the price was drastically different from the current day. The funeral home tried hard to add additional services to recoup some of their costs, but we stayed to the plan—direct cremation, remains in a white box that we would put in the church yard at the cathedral. No casket, no embalming, no frills. You could see their disappointment.

Mom had a beautiful nightgown and robe we dressed her in. We could not get her wedding ring off, but they were able to remove it and return to us. The funeral home asked if we wanted to have her gown back and we said no. It was a beautiful peignoir set she had purchased just before she married our stepfather. Both mom and her second husband had been widowed for years. We wanted her to wear the most luxurious, beautiful thing she owned. She deserved to arrive in heaven as the classy lady she was on earth in her beautiful peignoir. Mom's service was at the cathedral and the associate at the cathedral officiated at her service. I asked if I could carry the cremains to the garden instead of the acolyte. I was able to do that and place the cremains in the ground near my father's ashes.

I have recognized terminal restlessness in other patients, but why didn't I see it with my mom? I had released all supervision to the hospice team so I could be her daughter. I had created boundaries, and they were so strong that I was not "clinical" when I was "daughter" Beck. The hospice team also maintained boundaries for me. They did not call me to tell me about signs they were seeing until they had obvious proof. I do not think Mom had any idea that she was dying until she woke up on Sunday morning. The nurses were so good because, when they realized what was happening, they started medication for anxiety. It was wonderful to make sure Mom was calm and not anxious and that she would not be in any pain. The minute they gave Mom anxiety medicine, and she was in bed, she was able to relax. Only on Sunday morning around 10:15 a.m. had the hospice nurses realized Mom was dying. There were signs in her feet, on her legs, or hands that told them she was dying.

In terminal restlessness the spirit is letting go. I am more and more of the feeling that terminal restlessness is the human spirit and the Holy Spirit in conversation before the person intellectually or emotionally realizes what is happening. In terminally restless patients you may not see the usual signs of the dying process right away.

My mom died on December 14, 2016. She was ninety-five years old. My mom was surrounded by her family holding hands, singing, talking, telling stories, sharing their love. It was a peaceful, quiet, and holy death. This experience led me to write the book "The Birthing of a Spirit." My mom's death made me think about how we celebrate new life coming into the world, but we also need to celebrate a life well lived. Mom earned her master's degree at the age of sixty. Mom had been a widow for over ten years when she remarried, at age sixty-five. Mom fell in love with a man she had known since 1949. They dated briefly and had eight wonderful and happy years traveling and splitting time between Maine and Missouri. Countless moments and memories existed in between. My mom lived a full life!

— Chapter 37 —

Baptismal Grace

MANY OF MY HOSPICE patients are in nursing homes. This patient was a single woman in her fifties who was a very large woman, weighing probably 450 pounds, and required an extra-large bed. Bless her heart, she was uncomfortable, just miserable every single day. All day long she would scream and yell out to anyone who would listen. There was nothing that anyone could do to make her more comfortable. She was angry and frustrated with her life.

I went to visit her every week and I could always hear her screaming before I got to her room. I told her several times that God loved her, and she was God's precious child no matter what she held in her mind or heart. She was forgiven. However, she still screamed and screamed and screamed. I asked if I could do something to help her, and she always said no. After a few visits I left with an idea. I called the priest at our church and asked, if I baptized someone at one of my facilities, could I list the baptism with them because a baptism has to be listed with a church to be official. He said yes, that would be fine, so I moved forward with my idea.

My next visit was on a Friday afternoon. I went in to see her at my usual time, and as before she continued screaming as I walked into her room. I stood at the side of her bed and called her by name. When she turned her attention to me, I asked her if she had been baptized and, if not, if she would like to be. She said that she had not and would very much like to be baptized. I let her know that I could baptize her that day, in her room. I let her know that I talked to the priest at our church and her name would be in the baptismal record at that Episcopal church. Curious, she asked what "Episcopal" was. We went on to talk about how Episcopal was like Roman Catholic, but it wasn't. Episcopal is an English Catholic or an Anglo-Catholic church. She nodded her acknowledgment as I shared more details. After answering her questions, I excused myself to gather a few things and asked her to wait there patiently for me to return. I went to the activities desk and let them know I needed a witness for baptism. The activities director volunteered but was skeptical about why I was doing this. I went to the kitchen and asked for a small bowl with a little water. I removed the blessed oil from my bag. The oil was a healing oil. It was not the usual oil for baptism, but it was worthy of the occasion. This lady needed to feel the full gift of baptism and God's and Jesus's love for her. On my way back to the patient's room, I stopped to let the director of nursing know what I was doing and that I would add the baptism to my part of the patient's chart. I also called the patient's daughter to let her know what we were going to do so that she was not surprised. She gave her blessing.

The activities director and I went into the patient's room carrying the small bowl with water, some paper towels, and the blessed oils. I stood on one side of the bed, and the director was on the other side. I told the patient I was going to baptize her, and the activities director was there to be the witness to the baptism. I also let her know that I had spoken to her daughter, and she gave her blessing. The patient nodded and agreed to continue.

I took the water and said to the patient, "I baptize you in the name of the Father, and of the Son, and of the Holy Spirit." I then took the oil and said to her, "I make the sign of the cross on your forehead reminding you that you are sealed as Christ's own forever." I reminded her that God will, if you ask, forgive all your sins. She was silent and her eyes were closed. As I concluded the baptism, I let her know she was a precious child of God, loved by Him, and saved by his grace. I thanked her and said it was an honor to baptize her. I let her know I was going to step out to call the priest to share her name and age to be added to the church record. I said goodbye and ended my visit for that day and let her know I would see her again next week. She remained silent and calm as I left the room.

I got a call on Monday that she had passed away. The nurse told me that after she was baptized, she never made another sound. The screaming and the outbursts of anger and frustration had ended. The nurse jokingly asked if I could go around and baptize several others! It was amazing to learn that she never made another sound, after screaming every moment for six weeks. The power of the Holy Spirit never ceases to amaze me. The Holy Spirit, she is good!

Life had not been good to this woman, and it was not a happy thing for her to carry that anger and frustration. I am convinced that she had done some things for which she needed to be forgiven. She needed to hear she was a precious child of God and was saved by God's grace. She needed the outward and visible signs of the inward and spiritual grace of baptism. She needed to know she was sealed as Christ's own forever and that God would forgive her of all her sins. Through baptism, her spirit was set free.

— Chapter 38 —

A Note about Grief

THE DEATH OF A loved one is a life-changing experience! The grief we feel is real. Your grief can manifest itself in many ways. Grief is as individual as the history and life experience of the person grieving. Some health care professionals refer to the person who is grieving as *grievers*. I am not fond of that term. Why? Because grief can appear to take over a life, but it does not become the whole person; grief is always only a part of who we are, a part of our beautiful spirit!

We grieve many things during a lifetime; but the grief I want to talk about is the grief when someone we love dies (a longtime friend or loved one). Grief comes from deep emotion. When we are grieving, it will be harder when we deny the feelings that come with grief. Grief can manifest itself in overcompensation and being lost in busy work. Grief can live in swallowed anger. This anger can be dangerous. Why? Because with swallowed anger we hurt our body and we can lash out unexpectedly without thinking to those our spirit considers safe.

Of course, there are many more ways grief can manifest. Tears and red eyes are the most common. Some of us cry out our grief. How about the denied grief? Your grief will come out even if you put it in an emotional box in your spirit and say to yourself, "I will deal with it later."

After my father's death at fifty-five, I put my grief away and denied my grief. One Sunday morning, ten years after my father's death, I was sitting in "our pew" alone for the first time. Our girls had finished college and were well on their own. My husband and our two youngest children were serving in the service. And I realized I was sitting alone!

Just as the processional started, a longtime friend tapped me on the shoulder and simply said, "I remember how this hymn was your dad's favorite." That was all it took! I fought my tears for the first few minutes of the service. After church in a cleared parking lot, my husband and our two boys found me in the car still crying uncontrollably. When we got home, I went straight to bed and cried myself to sleep. The next morning, I felt like a weight was lifted from my shoulders. Grief comes out even if you try to hide your grief! Grief is a sign of love. We love family, friends, and even our dear pets. We grieve so many things.

As a chaplain I have a hard time when I hear someone say, "I know exactly how you feel." No one knows how another person feels. The statement sounds to me like someone is trying to steal my feelings. In my mind I know they aren't, and they mean well, but it is still a silly statement said when we don't know what else to say, and we feel we must say something.

The statement above makes as much sense to me as the older person who leans down to a child and says, "Oh, Honey, God loved her so much he took her home to be with him." I suspect the child thinks, "God, please don't love me too much because I want to be here!" As a hospice chaplain I have heard staff say so many times, "The family are grieving normally." So, what is normal? How can you, who just met me, know if I am grieving normally? We all have our own normal. But grief may bring tears. Grief may bring quiet or calm as the person grieving works though their own grief process. Grief may bring nervous energy and over-functioning. These are processes many people go through as they grieve a loved one dying. Professional help might be needed if the person grieving threatens to hurt themselves or others and if the deep soul grief lasts longer than six months. Receiving professional help is never a sign of weakness and should be supported by those in the grieving person's support system.

We never know what to say, and the silence can feel deafening. Sometimes we don't need words; we just need someone to listen to our pain. Hollow words are thrown around at funerals and celebrations of life like a wild ping pong ball. If you don't know what to say and you feel a great need to talk, then think about simply saying, "I am so sorry."

Remember, we all grieve differently, and my grief can't be your grief. We can't share feelings! Grief can't be graded as to how much you grieve. My grief for my mother's death at ninety-five was completely different from my grief for my dad who died at fifty-five. Dad had miles to go, though I believe Mom had a long, beautiful life.

So, who grades grief? A trained professional psychologist, perhaps! Not a person who just met you, someone who has no idea of your story, and not even people in your own family. When we are around a dramatic loss, it is a time to watch, listen, and be present. It is not a time for doing.

Now that you know my feelings about grief, let's talk about support for those who are grieving. There are a plethora of books about grief. If your loved one died while on hospice, this would be the time to call your hospice bereavement coordinator for recommendations. If you are close to a person who is the pastoral care support of a clergy team, that would be a good call for recommendations as well. You can also consider a visit to your local bookstore.

You might be thinking about grief in a small child. I have found that a child grieving is as unique as that child. Please realize this is a time to play down the "going to heaven" card. Often this can scare the young child or teenager. When I have been asked to talk with a child about a parent or grandparent's death, I do lots of praying first! You need to know about that child; don't just step in without preparation. Over the years I have been surprised how the simplest book can intrigue children from five years to teenagers. Simple is good. There is no need to make this conversation complicated.

When you come in love with a peaceful spirit, your audience will respond. I can't tell you how many conversations I have started with children on one end of the sofa and me on the other, and, as I read, the child or teenager ended up next to me looking over my shoulder or in my lap. This is a time for your low inside voice; read slowly and distinctively and listen.

Conclusion

THANK YOU FOR READING my stories and our book! So, how do you get to be a hospice patient? Your medical professional will be the person to share with you and those you hold dear about hospice. You will hear the doctor say, "Victor, at the rate your illness is progressing I think it is time we called in a hospice team." Now, this is when you take a deep breath and realize the "death angel" is *not* at the door. But it is time to get your affairs in order and to enjoy every moment you have with those you care most about.

I have always thought I would rather have time to talk to my family and dear friends before it is time to make the sacred journey. As a hospice chaplain, I have spent my share of time on the freeway. Dying on the freeway is not on my list of things to do. My list includes sharing with my spouse and children and talking with those I have known for fifty plus years about how I love them. My siblings are very much on my list of conversations. They need to know the big sister is not leaving but just in another dimension.

So, you had your conversation with your medical professional; now what? It is highly likely you will be given a list of names and phone numbers for several hospice organizations. Please interview all the companies on the list you are given. This is not a time to take your neighbor's advice. Hospice organizations have personalities just like any other organization. You are going to find not-for-profit and for-profit hospices. Over the years I can't tell you how many times I have heard, "I am not going to have a for-profit hospice." Well, I am here to tell you every company must make a profit, or they can't deliver the services they advertise! Don't be fooled by the word "profit." Listen to the person you are interviewing. It is highly likely that they reflect the group of professionals they work with. The patient is the team leader and the hospice staff come to support you and your loved ones!

When you have your appointment interviews with each hospice, make a list of questions and ask a good friend to take notes. You and your loved ones are too involved to hear everything. A good notetaker is primary to your decision. You want to ask what services the hospice provides. By Medicare guidelines certain health care professionals are required to be part of the hospice care team. Most insurance agencies follow Medicare guidelines. Some hospice services offered by a hospice may be elective, such as a music therapist. Usually, the hospice team includes the following health care professionals: a registered nurse as the case manager, a social worker, a bath aide, and a chaplain. Be aware, hospice agencies have personalities that reflect their staff! All members of your team are important for you to receive the best care. Here is an example: "Did I hear you say we don't need a chaplain because your pastor/rabbi/imam will be visiting? Okay, but why not also have the trained chaplain visiting?" Your chaplain offers spiritual support. If the chaplain is a religious support, that is just gravy. No one is coming to convert you. The chaplain is fine where they are spiritually. The chaplain comes to support your spirituality, wherever you see God or don't see God. *We all have a spirit!* The spirit is the essence of who you are.

Over the years I have had some very deep conversations with patients, as they shared with me something very private that they hadn't shared with their pastor. A hospice chaplain follows the principle "What happened in Vegas stays in Vegas." Why? Well, a chaplain can go away and not come back. But be aware your chaplain has a professional education and he/she is trained to walk with you and your family as you progress through the dying process. The chaplain, like anyone on your hospice team, can help answer your questions or reach out to your team member who can best answer your question. Just as an obstetrician is trained to deliver babies, so each member of the hospice team does their part to deliver your spirit peacefully into eternity.

Your entire hospice team will be medically trained professionals. But you are the team captain! Your family will need the team's support just as well as you. Grief comes to everyone experiencing hospice. Your hospice will have a bereavement coordinator. This person will hear about you and your family at the biweekly team meetings, and the bereavement coordinator will be ready to support your family. Your team will also include the hospice director of nursing and a medical director. Your information is protected by the Health Insurance Portability Accountability Act (HIPAA), like patients in any other medical situation.

I suspect you would not take a trip to a new area of the country without a map, so why would you start this holy and sacred journey without the trained guides who have helped many patients and their loved ones make this sacred and holy journey? Your hospice team will help you live your dying to the fullest, trying to not waste a moment!

So, is there a heaven? *Yes!* I don't know what the next level of existence is, but from the depths of my spirit I know it is there! And for lack of a better word, I use "heaven."

God's peace to you. And again, thank you for reading this book.

About the Author

How It All Began

A DEACON IN THE Episcopal Church is very different from deacons in other Protestant denominations. In the Episcopal and Roman Catholic churches, deacons are similar; the one exception is women are ordained in the Episcopal Church. I have felt called to ordination since I was fourteen years old, and I believe the culmination of my life experiences ultimately led me to this path. I used to laugh at others who said they had "a call," mocking them for having a direct line to God. But I realized later it was easier to laugh than it was to admit I had a calling as well. I just could not answer it at the time. It was not until the hospital I worked at closed that I felt free to follow my call. God works in mysterious ways. It so happened that I could not find the same level of job in the community because I had not completed my undergraduate degree. It was then, at the age of forty-eight, that I had the opportunity to complete my undergraduate studies and request a meeting with my parish priest for approval to be an aspirant for ordination.

As I embarked on my coursework, I did not dare tell anyone what I had in mind to do after completing my degree, not even my husband. The reason was that historically in my life I was really good at sharing my dreams, but then, once I had shared them aloud, I no longer felt like I had to go after those dreams. But this time, I held my dream close so I could hold my own feet to the fire and make it a reality. I needed to know I could do it on my own without anyone helping me before I invited others in. I knew that I needed to complete my degree before I could go to my priest and bishop to move forward as an aspirant to ordination, so I decided to take it one step at a time.

After I completed my courses and was preparing to graduate, I invited my husband to lunch. As soon as we were seated, Bob asked me why we were there and the intent of my invitation. Diving straight into the deep end, I shared that I thought I would go to the bishop to initiate the process for ordination. His eyes got wide, and he seemed to slump down like he was going to slide out of the booth! He was floored and disappointed that I had not shared my goals sooner. Looking back, I could easily understand, because Bob had already been there himself. He had been to seminary, had his masters of divinity degree, and had been a Presbyterian pastor. In that moment his wife of twenty years was saying she wanted to start a second career and pursue ordination. In the end, I had his complete support and continued my pursuit.

One of the steps was for Bob and me to attend a weekend event where I would be interviewed by two laypersons and two priests who would be making recommendations as to whether I was a good candidate for ordination. The day prior to the weekend I had requested an emergency meeting with the bishop. I implored him that this event would be all about priesthood; I knew I would be required to go away to seminary and I knew I would never leave my family to go to seminary. The bishop said he believed my call was to be a priest, but I insisted I wasn't called to leave my family and there had to be another way to be ordained. He finally agreed and asked if I had read the "Ordination to the Diaconate." I admitted I had not because I did not want to read it until I knew whether I could do it. Flippantly, I shared that it felt like I would be going to the bakery and smelling the fresh bread without knowing if I would be able to eat it! Why would I torture myself like that? He excused himself and stepped out to call the interim priest at my church, St. Paul's. (Ironically, his name was Paul, which seemed fitting for a man named Father Paul to be a priest at a church called St. Paul's.) The bishop returned and immediately instructed me to leave his office and head straight to St. Paul's to speak with Father Paul. I looked at him quizzically, and he said not to question him but to do as he was instructing. It was imperative if I wanted to be ordained.

I went straight to St. Paul's and checked in with Father Paul. He picked up his prayer book and came around his desk and sat next to me. Father

Paul opened his prayer book to the "Ordination to the Diaconate" and insisted I read it. Just as with the bishop, I scoffed and pushed it away. He ignored my attitude, saying he had watched me engage in the church and felt this was where I was called. He went on to share that I had described wanting to be out in the world among the people. He explained that was exactly what a deacon was called to do: to go forth into the world and to send the congregation out every Sunday morning "to go in peace and love and serve the Lord." To me, being a chaplain seemed to be one of the best ways to answer my call. To me, being a priest meant to be a "ruler," and that just wasn't me. The more I immersed myself in the ordination process, the more conviction I had that I had been called to be a chaplain. Father Paul communicated with the bishop, and I had received the blessing of my church and the bishop to take the next step.

Bob and I went to the weekend event. Throughout the long conversations I shared why I felt called to be ordained and the passion I felt to be a deacon. The committee argued that I should do priesthood versus diaconate. One of the priests even said he would vote "no" because he did not think I was called to the diaconate. But, my first call was to my husband, Bob, and motherhood with our four children. God would not ask me to leave them for three years of seminary out of state away from our home.

At the time I thought this was kind of funny because my father had been an Episcopal priest, and his last assignment prior to his death was Dean of Grace and Holy Trinity Cathedral in Kansas City. Ten years after my father's death, my mother married our former and retired bishop, the same man who ordained the first female Episcopal priests. I got a lot of push-back that I needed to be ordained as a priest rather than a deacon. I was told my father would not be happy if I were to be a deacon and not a priest. I had to keep saying that it was not my father who was being ordained, it was me. Dad had chosen his path, and this was my path. I remember how my father felt about deacons. Like how he would have grown with women's ordination to the priesthood, he would have grown and agreed with my ordination as a deacon and being a chaplain. He would have been proud.

My response today if my father were here would be that I am a hospice chaplain and I do have a congregation. They are just a little more mobile, of many faiths, and more spread out, than a traditional congregation. I can go to where my congregation is versus them coming to me in a church. My father passed away before the national church approved women's ordination. My stepfather was the bishop who ordained female priests before it had been approved by the national church. Dad had once said he had no problem with women being ordained; he would just wait until it was approved and in the rubrics of the prayer book. He believed we had the rules for a reason and did not believe in breaking them for your own beliefs.

Ultimately, I did get a vote of "yes" from the committee and was officially an aspirant to ordination. But to become a full-time chaplain, I needed to enroll in a yearlong Clinical Pastoral Education (CPE) training program. Since I was going through the ordination process, I wanted to join the CPE program at the Episcopal hospital in town. I was deeply offended when I was turned away from their program and was instead assigned to the Baptist hospital across town. As an Episcopalian I thought it was important for me to learn and grow among the community I knew so well. I did not know what to think until my friend explained to me that I would never develop my pastoral identity meeting people I already knew. I could not deny their point of view but was concerned about what a pastoral identity was and how I would find it, especially at a Baptist hospital. Thirty years ago for me, it was a big deal to be an Episcopal chaplain doing stand-up prayer in a Baptist hospital. Episcopalians were never known for their stand-up prayer. Before I started CPE my mother laughed about how I was going to learn stand-up prayer, also known as a heart prayer, at the Baptist hospital. This is the silent prayer you say to yourself when you need instant help. And my mother was right. I learned it in an instant with the help of the Holy Spirit.

Normally in the ordination process you would take one quarter of CPE, but to be a board certified chaplain (BCC) requires four quarters and a master of divinity degree. It was no easy task. Aside from working all hours of the day and night and being on call, the CPE program was a huge challenge on its own because you must face all your own "stuff." And let's be honest, no one likes owning or confronting their own "stuff." CPE is emotionally and mentally exhausting while also physically demanding. On top of that, the Baptist hospital, where I was assigned for CPE, was one of the most confrontational CPE programs in the Midwest. Why? Because the head of the program was a man with a strong personality and presence. I remember a day, right after the first quarter of CPE, where I had done something that he perceived as "horrible." As a result, he pulled me into his office and positioned his chair right up against the front of my knees, skimming my shins. He leaned forward into my face and just yelled at me! I had had enough. I pushed him back, stood up, and stormed out with all my boundaries securely in place. I immediately grabbed a box on the way to my desk and packed my belongings and left for home. He did call me later to apologize, sharing he had just received some bad news, so he had reason for anger but no reason to take it out on me. I did go back to the program. Standing up to the director of the program was one of the most freeing moments of my life. To stand up and say I did not have to tolerate this and did not have to be there was freeing. The supervisor taught me a wonderful lesson. I learned to believe in myself and have the courage to stand firm. I believe the Holy Spirit taught us both that day.

No one else from my class stayed longer than the required amount of time, but I joked that I was not "cooked yet" and wanted more time to develop my pastoral identity. Everyone thought I was crazy because it was so hard, but I loved it so much that I stayed for seven quarters.

My children have met at least one, if not several, colleagues who tell them stories about their mom. They say their mom is so calming at the deathbed and her presence is quiet and peaceful. The kids were always astounded, thinking no way was their mom calm and peaceful. To one of my children it sounded like my colleagues were talking about an angel, and they really saw me "differently" at home. They saw a working and busy mom managing a seventeen-year age span across her four children. When we were home, we were a busy, funny, involved family engaging in everyone's school and social activities. It is amazing to me how my kids described me at home. In my work as a chaplain, I had peace at the deathbed because I was not the mother, I was the chaplain. At home, I was wife, mother, and hostess. When I get home, I take my "chaplain clothes" off before I go to my "wife and mother calling." It is necessary for me to take one call off to answer the other call.

I was one of the first Episcopal deacons to be a board certified chaplain in the Association of Professional Chaplains. As mentioned previously, you need a masters of divinity to be certified, but I qualified with my under-graduate degree, seven quarters of CPE, and my studies at the West Missouri School for the Diaconate. I began this journey in 1993, and by 1995 I was ordained as a deacon and was a board certified chaplain. Later, in 2003, I completed an Interdisciplinary Master's in Spirituality and Aging with a cer-tificate in Gerontology at the University of Missouri, Kansas City.

God's Mysterious and Wondrous Ways

THIS IS A LESSON in how God is part of all religious traditions. In this story, God showed me he not only works through all our religious traditions, but he also works in mysterious and wondrous ways. This story is also about my personal experience as a patient and as a person learning to follow God's lead.

I was about three months into a new job at a Seventh Day Adventist hospital. On a Tuesday, also my eighty-ninth day of work in my new chaplaincy, I was visiting patients at a nursing home. While I was standing at the nurse's station doing my patient charting, I was holding on to the counter so hard my knuckles were white. The nurse standing nearby looked at me and said I needed to see my doctor immediately. She said the last couple of weeks they had noticed me holding on to the nurse's station counter like I was going to fall. I didn't realize that and apologized. My left leg had been hurting and I did not know why. I just kept thinking the pain would go away, but it was getting worse and, clearly, I was not hiding it better.

I called the spiritual care office to tell them I checked out and went straight to my family physician's office. When I arrived, I told reception I did not have an appointment but would wait until I could be seen. The only person who could see me was a senior resident. I sat down with her and learned she had been a nurse in oncology before going to medical school. When she pressed on my stomach the pain was sharp. She said she needed to admit me immediately to run a series of tests. The next day, they did the tests, and late in the morning an older doctor came into my room with two residents. He looked over my tests and he did not see a problem that pain medications couldn't handle. He felt that my pain wasn't what the senior resident thought it was, and he would be sending me home. Right after that the senior resident came into my room and said they had looked at everything and wanted to do a colonoscopy. And so I started the prep for a Thursday morning colonoscopy.

When I woke up from the colonoscopy in the recovery room, the doctor came in and, without introducing himself, looked at me and said, "Mrs. Schubert, you have a large malignant tumor in your colon." And with that he turned around and left.

My husband, Bob, was in the car driving to the college where he was scheduled to teach. They had tried to call him, but he did not answer. It was in a time when mobile phones used to be on the floor of your car in a large box-shaped case. Bob called the oncologist back and heard the news

I had just been given. I had a large malignant tumor in my colon. What? How is this possible, we wondered? The doctor said they would schedule my surgery for the next afternoon (Friday) when they knew the operating room was available. I told her there was a surgeon that I really liked and wanted for my surgery. She said she would call him right away. We needed to move quickly, so the arrangements were made. I remember in my mind shouting for God to hear, "What?! I just spent two years doing training, I have just been ordained, I started a new job, and now you are giving me a malignant tumor in my colon? Come on God, what is this?" Everyone had left my room by the time we had our talk.

It took my husband, adult children, and our son-in-law time to gather at the hospital. My son-in-law was first to arrive, and he came running into the room and gave me a kiss on my cheek and a hug. I was in tears. Then his wife, my daughter, arrived and my other daughter arrived. My husband arrived last, coming in after his class. He did ask if he should skip the class, but I said he should carry on; we needed the money and there was time to come later.

I was in the hospital where I had done my two years of training, so I had developed some really great relationships with staff across the hospital. The nurse manager of oncology called an oncologist I had worked with over the last two years. Before my surgery, the head of nursing in oncology even came to see me and said they were going to get me set up for some trial treatment programs. I did get into at least two programs. When they took me down to the operating room for my surgery, the entire waiting room was full of our friends! I remember how blessed I felt to have these dear family members and friends nearby as I had surgery. Our oldest son, who had just started driving, went home with his younger brother and best friend to play Legos all night. Just as they were getting ready to wheel me into the operating room, I heard, "Wait, wait! You can't take her yet!" In jeans, tennis shoes, and a plaid shirt, the former bishop, who was a dear friend of my father's and my spiritual director, came running down the hall. "You can't take her! Wait!" I was literally halfway through the doorway of the operating room with half of me hanging in the hallway when the doctors and nurses stopped the gurney. The bishop literally pushed his way in, saying he had to lay hands on me. He laid his hands on me, prayed, anointed me, and then allowed the team to take me. I do not know who called the bishop and how he knew I was there.

When they opened me up the tumor was completely encapsulated. The doctor that did the colonoscopy said he could see the tumor was outside the colon wall. But when they went in, nothing was outside or in the colon wall. The tumor was encapsulated inside the wall of my colon. It was great news.

I had called my boss, the head of the chaplaincy department at the medical center, to share my diagnosis and that I was at another hospital for surgery. Somehow the news made its way to the personnel department. To his surprise, the personnel department immediately terminated my employment. Turns out, I was admitted to the hospital on my eighty-ninth day of employment. By terminating me on my eighty-ninth day, they would not have to provide my full health coverage and benefits that were set to begin on my ninety-first day of employment. The worst part? I didn't know. No one notified the chaplaincy department or me that I had been terminated, and now effective on day ninety I no longer had any benefits. I did not learn of my termination until I was out of the hospital, when my paycheck didn't arrive.

The chaplaincy department called me and said that the personnel department terminated me because I was in the hospital on my eighty-ninth day and they knew I would be off and not be able to work my ninety days to have full coverage. They said maybe when I was better, I could come back. When the head of the chaplaincy department found out, he was so chagrined that he went to the hospital administrator at the medical center to share what happened. He let them know of my hospitalization and that on my ninetieth day, without contacting me, they terminated my employment. When the president of the hospital learned what happened, he was infuriated. He wrote me an apology letter on behalf of the entire hospital. In his letter he reinstated me, paid me for the six weeks I was off recovering, and held my job for me until I was ready to return. He also said that they would cover my insurance. What a precious gift. But my story does not end here. This is one of those times when I say God works in mysterious ways, his wonders to perform amaze me.

My surgery was at the end of August, and I was off the entire month of September and part of October. When I got back to work in mid-October, all the of the chaplains were called in together. There were several of us, and, unfortunately, they let us know they had to downsize the group, and the two newest chaplains were given notice. Another Episcopal chaplain and I were the ones being let go, and we had two weeks to find new jobs. A few days later, I ran into one of the oncology nurses I knew from my time in training when she was a student nurse, and we had both started at the same time. I was there to celebrate with her when she passed her nursing boards. She now wondered what I was doing as chaplain at the hospital. After working with me as an oncology chaplain and as the AIDS clinic chaplain, she saw me as a death and dying chaplain. She was heading to work for a hospice and thought I needed to be a hospice chaplain. She wanted me to join the company with her. There was only one chaplain there and, surely, they needed two, she thought. She was very encouraging and got me an appointment to talk to her boss. She had no idea I was losing my job. God works in mysterious ways.

I went into the interview and sat down across from a man I knew from many years ago, before I became a chaplain. He was a salesman who called on my office when I was wearing scrubs working as the director of the central services department at a hospital in town. I asked him how he was sitting across from me, so he shared that he and some others came together to start a for-profit hospice business and he was now in charge of operations. In turn, he wanted to know how I got to be a chaplain. I shared my story and told him I needed a job. Without a beat he said he had a job for me, and could I start Monday? Wow, thank you!

Two years later, when the owners decided to break up their business, I was looking for a new job again. I was then offered a part-time chaplain job at a local Episcopal hospital. To fill the other half of my time, the director of spiritual care, a friend of mine, helped me get a part-time job at a for-profit ventilatory hospital. It was the toughest duty I have ever done. I continued to balance both jobs for eighteen months, when God had a new plan. Out of the blue, I got a call from the bishop's office. The bishop was asking to have lunch with me, and I could not imagine why. I did not have time to have lunch between my two jobs, so had to request to leave work early to meet him.

The bishop requested that I be his assistant while his current assistant transitioned to assisting the new incoming bishop. I believed it should be easy for me to do since I was familiar with the diocese. Looking back, I never questioned why the bishop asked me. I accepted his offer, but I only lasted in that role from March to December. I had to admit to the bishop that being his assistant was not where I was meant to be. I felt empowered when the new bishop asked me what in the world I was doing there. He said I was clearly a chaplain, not an assistant. He told me I was a chaplain and I needed get back out into the world. I agreed. My spirit felt a great need to be a chaplain again. I did not enjoy what I was doing and no longer knew why I was there.

With perfect timing, I was told that a long-term care facility owned by the Sisters of St. Joseph of Carondelet was looking for a chaplain. The executive director, whom I had met before, invited me in for an interview. She was lovely and it felt like good interview. I felt comfortable speaking with her, and our interaction felt very natural. Soon after, she called me back for a second interview. I walked into a room with eight people around a large table with a single open chair for me. Questions came from around the room, but I felt really relaxed the entire time. I enjoyed my time with the group. One of those in the group was a priest. I left thinking it was a great interview, but they were never going to hire a woman wearing a clerical collar at a Catholic facility. When I walked out of the conference room there was a nun sitting there waiting for her turn to interview. I introduced myself and told her she would be great in the job. She shared her name, and I said I would keep her in my prayers, and she was going to be a great chaplain. Thinking it was great but never expecting to be called back and hired, I did not hear anything for a few days. Then the executive director called to thank me for interviewing. I let her know I really enjoyed the interview process and the opportunity to practice my interviewing. I shared that I enjoyed meeting everyone and thought the meetings were great. After a pause she chuckled. I was confused; I did not really understand her phone call. She interrupted me and said she was trying to hire me and wanted to know if that would be okay. "Umm, yes! That would be great, thank you!" I told her. I honestly believed there was no way they would hire me. God's mysterious and wondrous ways!

It was the end of December, and the executive director wanted me to come to the facility's Christmas party to meet all staff, residents, and family members. She said that the nun I was replacing had already left, so it would be great to have me come in. I went to the facility for the party. While I was there, I went around introducing myself to the residents and their families. There was one family that had gathered in the private dining room. I stepped in to introduce myself and wished them a wonderful holiday. One of the daughters followed me out of the room and said, "Please leave my mother alone. You are not a Roman Catholic and we do not believe in you as the new chaplain." Wow. Her message was clearly received, and I would not be interacting with them again. Interestingly, I always saw their mother in the hallway and would stop to talk. There was no reason for me to be rude and not engage in conversation when she would initiate conversation with me. Over time, she and I became very good friends. The daughter and I also became friends along with the rest of the family. She apologized many times for their first introduction to me. It was a wonderful two years growing with them and the others at this facility. God opens doors for all religious traditions.

God's plan for me was changing again. I was asked to apply for a chaplain's position at our main hospital. I would be assigned to ICU and emergency room. This area had been the responsibility of a priest who was called back into parish ministry. I wondered what it would be like to follow a priest in the hospital; it was an interesting trip! The nurses were delightful, warm, and welcoming. The patient families were good to me as well. I remember there was a patient who was surprised when he realized I was wearing a clerical collar. The first day I met him I had worn a light blue shirt with my clerical collar. The next time I visited with him, I walked into the room wearing a dark blue clerical shirt and my white collar was very visible against the dark blue.

The patient was on oxygen with a major heart challenge. He looked at me and said, "I knew it! I told my wife you were wearing a clerical collar and now I know you are! How did you get into a Catholic hospital?" I smiled. My response was simple: "I am a chaplain, and I was hired." We had a nice conversation about it. I enjoyed the time I served as chaplain at that institution.

After five years I returned to hospice. While at the hospital I started to realize how much I missed having a congregation. Yes, long-term care had been like a congregation. Many times hospice patients are with us for six months or more. Hospice chaplaincy is serving a congregation; they are just more "mobile than a church congregation." My heart sings and is so at peace when I can be present with many families as their loved ones make the sacred journey from this life to the next.

Throughout my time as chaplain, I have tried to follow God's plan. It was often mysterious but always wondrous. My journey in the ICU led me through many different religious traditions, and each offered rich food for thought to this Christian. What I experienced as I ministered to many Christian traditions, Muslim, Buddhist, Hindu, and non-religious families gave me spiritual food for thought.

Resources and Additional Information

A Note about Prayer Beads

FORMS OF PRAYER BEADS have been used for centuries by many religions, including Hindus, Jews, and Muslims. It was around AD 600 when the church realized that because many people did not read as the clergy did, they believed people needed some way to pray. The rosary was then created so that people could use memorized prayer with the beads. The Roman Catholic rosary has five divisions, or decas, but my prayer beads have only four decas. Some prayer beads have Christian symbols like a cross or a circle, which is a sign of God's unending love. They are also made using many different colors, materials such as glass, wood, or even metal, and varying types of beads.

The prayer beads I shared with people consist of a cross, or a large "invitatory bead" and then a small loop of thirty-three beads divided into four groups. The four groups contain seven beads with additional beads of a different color or size that separate the groups. Counting the invitatory bead, the number thirty-three signifies the number of years Christ lived on the earth, while the number seven signifies the days of creation.

There are formal and informal ways to use prayer beads in prayer and meditation. But it is important to know they can be used in any way that brings you peace and comfort. Life has enough rules. There is no right way to pray, only your way. The beads are always small, making them just the right size to be snuggled in your hand. They also fit nicely in a pocket.

A Note on Spreading Ashes

Whenever someone says they are going to take their loved one's ashes somewhere, I always ask them to check the wind, check the way they are going to pour the ashes. Consider having a watering can with you, and if there is any wind, you get the bag down low on top of the target, even if you have to let the bag go with the ashes. People always look and I can see them thinking, Why is this lady sharing so much? But I assure them they need to think this through. Spreading ashes can go from a sacred and loving gesture to nightmare in an instant. I tell everyone. I tell them all whether they are going to the ocean, backyard, lake, or graveside. And I am *now* telling you.

A Note on Advance Directives

Advance Directives can be a legal document that allows patients to convey personal decisions about their care ahead of time. They provide a means to communicate their wishes to family, friends, and health care professionals and ensure their wishes are carried forward in the absence of their ability to direct their own care. Advance care planning can be delicate and vary for each one of us, but what is most important to stay focused on is ensuring the treatment plan aligns with the patient's and the family's values, beliefs, and wishes. Chaplains can be a great resource to provide prayer and spiritual support as you make your care decisions.

Several things to consider: Does your family know what you want if you can't tell them? Do your family members agree? If one child is not in agreement, then the physician may follow what they feel is best. Yes, this is very important. Many physicians do not have to follow the patient's request if the family is not in agreement. Check your state guidelines for an Advance Directive. Many states require your Advance Directive to be notarized. If you live on a state line it is smart to prepare for both state guidelines. An example: The state of Missouri requires an Advance Directive to be notarized but Kansas does not.

Every few years it is important to update your Advance Directive. If your medical challenges change, maybe your thoughts on sustaining life have changed. Keep a copy of your Advance Directive in your car's glove compartment in case of a wreck. It is smart to have a copy in your wallet or purse. Give a copy to everyone you have listed as an agent. Put the original in your safety deposit box. Never carry your original; what if it gets lost?

While we are on the subject, how is your will? Do you have someone else on your checking account in case you can't sign checks? Where are your passwords stored? And several people need to know where the important papers are kept. It is hard to think of our demise, but it is not only necessary, it is smart!

A Note about Hospice

It is time for hospice when your physician says to you, "At the rate your disease is progressing I think it is time to add the hospice team to your care." Your physician will normally refer your name and information to several hospice organizations. If you live in a small town, you may only have one hospice. Here is a list of the positions that make up many hospice teams. Also below is a list of suggested questions for the hospice interview. Remember to have someone take notes. And, finally, we have included several websites where you will find even more hospice information.

Your Hospice Team and How They Function

The patient is always considered the team leader! The patient and their family become a priority for the hospice team. Your entire team sees their work as "holy." Very rarely does someone come to be part of the hospice team if they don't feel a "call" to this area of medicine.

The medical director reviews and certifies all patients with the team every two weeks. The medical director is usually a physician in the community who has experience with hospice.

The case manager is a registered nurse who has had experience and training with treating patients who have a terminal diagnosis. You will find as you get to know your nurse that they are a great resource for your questions and an advocate for your loved one. All questions are welcome, and your nurse loves to share. The nurse will visit several times a week and will present your loved one's information at the team meeting every two weeks.

The social worker will usually visit twice a month and helps you access all support in your area. The social worker will likely ask about burial plans and assist in accessing what best fits your wishes. Also, he/she will ask about an Advance Directive and assist you with completing yours. The visit may include hearing your story, reading to you, and playing the style of music you like.

The chaplain usually visits twice a month. The chaplain comes to offer spiritual support and a quiet presence. The chaplain *never* evangelizes; he/she is fine where they are and they have come to support you where you are spiritually. The chaplain may ask if you would like them to call your congregation. Many chaplains will sing with you, read to you, listen to your life story, and, of course, if you would like, the chaplain will pray with you in the style of prayer you prefer. The chaplain will also officiate at the Celebration of Life for your loved one, if needed. The goal for the chaplain is to be a quiet, supportive presence to you and your loved ones.

The bath aide comes to help with personal care and usually visits twice a week. The duties of the bath aide vary with the hospice. Ask the hospice about the duties of the bath aide.

The director of volunteer services recruits and trains volunteers according to hospice and the guidelines of your state. Hospice volunteers' duties vary with the gifts of the volunteer. You may have a volunteer who reads, comes to listen, plays the violin. Volunteers often work in the hospice office.

The bereavement coordinator will be contacting the family and loved ones of the patient after the death. The bereavement coordinator will call the family and offer support for their grief for eighteen months after the death of the patient. The duties of the bereavement coordinator vary with the hospice, but usually you will have support calls every few months just checking in, and you will receive supportive care. Most hospice organizations have an annual memorial service where all patients who have died in the last year are celebrated. The hospice staff will celebrate those lives with you.

The nurse practitioner reviews all cases and at the end of each certification period they do patient evaluations. Don't be surprised if the nurse practitioner makes a visit.

Additional Hospice Team Members

The hospice team members below may be added by your hospice team, but they are not part of the core team. I have found these specialties to be very beneficial.

The music therapist is a trained music therapist who comes to sit and play music of your choice.

The massage therapist is trained to offer a massage to the patient, focusing on helping with muscle pain caused by disease or by lack of physical activity.

Suggested Questions for Your Interview with Hospice Representatives

Please remember there are no "silly" questions. Your concerns need to be addressed and your questions answered. I pray for you and each person making this sacred and holy journey and for those making the journey with hospice.

1. Who are the members of the care team?

2. May I keep my regular doctor?

3. How often do the team members visit?

4. How long can we have hospice?

5. I thought hospice was only for patients with cancer. Can you tell me more?

6. Will you take away the patient's medication?

7. My friend said her mom was discharged from hospice. Does that happen often?

8. How will you treat the patient's pain?

9. The patient doesn't want to eat—what do we do?

10. If the patient doesn't eat, will you give them a feeding tube?

11. What if we need you on a day you aren't visiting?

12. What if I need you in the middle of the night?

13. What if the patient wants to stay here in his own bed?

14. Does your team vigil with patients?

15. We are worried the patient could become addicted to the pain medicine.

National Organizations with More Information on Hospice

1. *National Association for Home Care and Hospice (NAHC).* Hospice resources developed for patients and families with the Center for Medicare Advocacy to assist you in this process.

2. *National Hospice and Palliative Care Organization (NHPCO).* The largest nonprofit membership organization represents hospice and palliative care programs and professionals.

3. *Center to Advance Palliative Care (CAPC).* National organization dedicated to increasing the availability of quality, equitable health care for people living with serious illness.

4. *Hospice Foundation of America (HFA).* Provides leadership in the development and application of hospice and its philosophy of care with the goal of enhancing the US health care system and the role of hospice within it.

Recommended Resources for Grief

The following is a list of additional resources on grief that I have shared with patients and families as well as resources I have used in my own life.

Books Recommended for Adults:

1. *A Grief Observed* by C. S. Lewis

2. *And Not One Bird Stopped Singing: Coping with Transition and Loss in Aging* by Doris Moreland Jones

3. *Getting to the Other Side of Grief: Overcoming the Loss of a Spouse* by Susan J. Zonnebell-Smeege and Robert C. DeVries

4. *Grief One Day at a Time* by Alan Wolfelt

5. *Healing after Loss: Daily Meditations for Working through Grief* by Martha Whitmore Hickman

6. *Healing a Spouse's Grieving Heart: 100 Practical Ideas after Your Husband or Wife Dies* by Alan D. Wolfelt

7. *I Heard the Owl Call My Name* by Margaret Craven

8. *I Wasn't Ready to Say Goodbye: Surviving, Coping and Healing after the Sudden Death of a Loved One* by Pamela Blair and Brook Noel

9. *Jesus: Miriam's Child, Sophia's Prophet* by Elisabeth Schüssler Fiorenza

10. *Love Is Stronger Than Death* by Peter Kreeft

11. *On Grief and Grieving: Finding the Meaning of Grief through the Five Stages of Grief* by Elisabeth Kubler-Ross, MD, and David Kessler

12. *Proof of Heaven: A Neurosurgeon's Journey into the Afterlife* by Dr. Eben Alexander

13. *Reaching Out* by Henri Nouwen

14. *Spiritual Care of the Dying* by Penelope Wilcock

15. *The Birthing of a Spirit: A Guide to a Holy and Sacred Death with Hospice* by Rebecca Malcolm Schubert

16. *Understanding Your Grief: Ten Essential Touchstones for Finding Hope and Healing Your Heart* by Alan D. Wolfelt

17. *You're Not Going Crazy—You're Grieving* by Alan D. Wolfelt

Books Recommended for Children and Teens:

1. *Grief Is Like a Snowflake* by Julia Cook and Anita DuFalla

2. *Tear Soup: A Recipe for Healing after Loss* by Pat Schwiebert and Chuck DeKlyen

3. *The Fall of Freddie the Leaf: A Story of Life for All Ages* by Leo Buscaglia, PhD

4. *The Invisible String* by Patrice Karst and Joanne Lew-Vriethoff

5. *Water Bugs and Dragonflies: Explaining Death to Young Children* by Doris Stickney and Gloria Claudia Ortez

Recommended Online Articles:

1. *Grief; It's Complicated* by Dana Sparks, Mayo Clinic, July 14, 2021. (This article is a good guide for when to call your clergy)

2. *Now What? Now We Learn From the Geese*, by Alan D. Wolfelt, Center for Loss and Life Transition, July 2021.

3. *What's Normal Grief? And How Does It Work?* by Alejandra Vasquez, The Cake Library—Coping with Grief, Updated August 6, 2021.

Bibliography

Episcopal Church. *The Book of Common Prayer and Administration of the Sacraments and Other Rites and Ceremonies of the Church, Together with the Psalter or Psalms of David, According to the Use of the Episcopal Church*. New York: Seabury, 1979.

Nouwen, Henri J. M. *Reaching Out*. New York: Doubleday, 1986.

Wilcock, Penelope. *Spiritual Care of Dying and Bereaved People*. London: Society for Promoting Christian Knowledge, 1996.